TEA: The Eyelids of Bodhidharma

Eelco Hesse

Tea:
The Eyelids of Bodhidharma

Prism Press

Published in Great Britain 1982 by

PRISM PRESS
Stable Court
Chalmington
Dorchester, Dorset DT2 0HB

Originally published by Uitgeverij Bert Bakker in Holland
Translated by First Edition and
published by agreement with Writers House, Inc.,
21 West 26 Street, New York 10010

ISBN 0 907061 05 2 (Hardback)
ISBN 0 907061 06 0 (Paperback)

CREDITS

Thanks are due to The Tea Council for their help and advice
and for providing the photographs of the London Tea Auction
and the modern tea factory.

Printed by
The Bowering Press Ltd, London

Contents

Introduction

'Thank God for tea! Where would the world be without tea? I am glad that I wasn't born before tea!' This famous statement made by the 18th century cleric Sydney Smith, seemed to me an eminently suitable opening for a book on tea in all its aspects.

Chapter 1 will deal with the arrival of tea in Europe and the New World and especially with the great tea drinkers of Europe—English, Dutch and Russians. There are romantic stories about the English smugglers and the race of the tea clippers as well as details of two historical events of importance in which tea played a special role: the famous Boston Tea Party, which was to lead to the independence of the United States, and the Opium Wars between Britain and China, which heralded the period of decline for the Middle Kingdom, from which the New China emerged.

In Chapter 2 we look at the role of tea in Chinese and Japanese cultures. Chapter 3, although not intended as a text book for tea planters, gives some information about the cultivation and processing of tea. Chapter 4 contains all sorts of data on the production and consumption of tea throughout the world and is followed in Chapter 5 by a list of all that is needed to brew a good cup of tea, plus the history of the tea service throughout the ages. Chapter 6 deals with the right way to brew tea and also gives a variety of recipes from Tibetan to iced tea.

Chapter 7 covers the pharmacological aspects of *Camellia Sinensis;* herb tea is dealt with in Chapter 8 and the latest developments in the tea trade in Chapter 9. Much has been said and written about tea and an anthology of quotes can be found in Chapter 10, with a list of useful addresses and a bibliography.

Ships of the Dutch East India Company in front of Canton in 1655. Competition started later.

Tea in Europe and the New World

The first European to inform the West about the existence of tea was Giambattista Ramusio, who published the travels in China of a Persian merchant, Haji Mahomet. In *Navigatione et Viaggi,* published in Venice in 1559, the Persian gave an account of the cultivation and preparation of tea. According to him, tea had all sorts of medicinal characteristics—even surpassing *rhubarb* in this respect! Trade with China had existed for a long time via the Arabian caravan route from Venice, but in the 16th century the Portuguese took over trade with China, this time by sea.

In 1557 Macao became Portuguese, and it is known that missionaries there tasted tea. Padre Matteo Ricci (1552–1610) an extraordinarily colourful figure, was an Italian missionary who found his way into the Imperial Court in Peking, where he held the position of scientific adviser. The accounts of tea in his letters reflect his technical outlook: he gives the price of tea in China and compares Chinese and Japanese methods of brewing.

At that time tea was not among the products that the Portuguese brought from the Orient to Europe, and which the Dutch then distributed throughout the continent. In 1595, the Portuguese closed their ports to the Dutch and from that time the Dutch began to build up their own power base in the East. Jan Huighen van Linschoten reported on tea drinking in Japan in 1595, and it was from Japan that the Dutch brought the first tea to Europe in 1610. This was green tea from the island of Hirado. The Dutch East India Company presented some of this tea to the princely court which set the fashion for tea drinking in Holland.

Trade with Japan was fraught with difficulties, however, and the Dutch were forced back to the small island of Decima. By now tea was becoming available from China. Initially it came in junks which brought it to the colony of Java. The Despatch Book of the Dutch East India Company stated on January 2nd 1637 that every ship from the East Indies was expected to bring Chinese as well as Japanese tea—a demand had obviously been created for it. In Holland the laxative qualities of the new exotic drink were recommended—an interesting thought. In general, it is striking that in the 17th century no real mention is made of the pleasant taste of tea but only of the various medicinal powers that tea was thought to possess. However, the method of transport was such that there was little hope of high quality tea arriving in Europe.

The Dutch government decided to send an

emissary to Canton and, as a result of this visit, received a letter from the Manchu emperor allowing them to trade, though under stringent conditions. The Dutch were to be allowed into China once every eight years with one hundred men of whom only twenty would be allowed at the Court. There were political reasons for the reserved attitude of the Manchu emperor— Southern China was rebelling against the central authorities and this area was not permitted to become too affluent. At least the door was now open for trade, with silk and tea as the most highly-prized products. The Dutch paid in silver because European commodities were of little value inside the Chinese Empire. The hoppo, a highly placed civil servant in charge of the tea trade in Canton, tried, with the aid of silver, to keep the authorities at court well-disposed towards him. Chinese merchants were dependent on the bene-volence of the hoppo as were the Portuguese, the Dutch and later the English.

Between 1660 and 1680 tea drinking in the Netherlands became more widespread. It was mostly consumed at home by the rich in special tea rooms, but gradually the habit was adopted by all social classes.

The medicinal effects of the new beverage were the subject of much controversy: the great Nicolaas Tulp was well-disposed towards the use of tea. It was an excellent remedy against gall stones, sleepiness and, diarrhoea, he claims in his *Observationes Medicae.* The world famous doctor, Cornelis Decker of Alkmaar, better known as Dr Bontekoe, published in the Hague in 1679 his *Treatise on the excellent herb Tea.* He sang the praises of tea to such an extent that he is suspected by some to have been on the payroll of the Dutch East India Company! The only thing that is certain is that afterwards he received a 'worthwhile presentation' for stimulating the use of tea in the Netherlands. The doctor had no objection to drinking as many as 200 cups.

In Holland tea was bought at the chemist where it was sold by the quarter. As the trade increased, the price came down, but there are stories of well-to-do families getting into financial difficulties through their tea parties. Remarkably, as early as the 17th century, the idea arose of cultivating tea in Indonesia, and in 1684 Dutch botanists conducted experiments on Java. However, the cultivation of tea in these areas was not established

Tea smuggling in England

until the 19th century. Not until 1878 were seeds finally imported from Assam and only then did the tea culture begin to flourish.

The history of tea in Russia is quite different from the West European. In 1567, Ivan Petrov and Boornash Yalyshev were the first Russian writers to mention the existence of tea. In 1638 an envoy was sent to the court of the Mongolian Khan. A gift of tea for Tsar Michael was refused since the Russian ambassador claimed his majesty had "no use for it". In 1689, Russia concluded the treaty of Nerchinsk with China, and tea began to arrive via the caravan route—an incredibly long journey through Mongolia and Siberia with every camel carrying about 600 lbs of tea. Tea drinking fast became fashionable at the court of the Romanovs. (The specifically Russian invention of the samovar and the tea glass will be discussed in a later chapter.)

The Germans and the French became familiar with tea through the Netherlands. The only part of Germany where tea drinking really caught on was East Friesland and the area around Bremen— elsewhere coffee and beer were preferred. In 1635, a Doctor Paulli from Rostock maintained that tea lost its mysterious powers outside the Orient and that in our climate it might even be dangerous. In France, conservative physicians united against the new beverage. A furore developed around Jean de Mauvillain's dissertation in favour of tea in the middle of 17th century and some doctors even went so far as to burn the manuscript. The title of the thesis was *'An the chinensium menti confert?'* (Does China tea improve the mind?). As far as the author was concerned this was a rhetorical question. The College de France showed itself to be a very conservative body by instigating a campaign against the promotor Dr Morissot.

Meanwhile, more favourable reports reached the French aristocracy from missionaries such as Alexandre de Rhodes. A second dissertation—this time by Pierre Cressy—*An Arthridi Thee Sinensium?* in 1657 met with fewer objections and slowly but surely the drink was accepted. French nationalists pointed to various herb extracts which had been drunk for centuries and which had suddenly been given the title of tea: sage and camomile for instance. Nicolas de Blegny reminded Louis XIV that in China and Japan nobody was plagued by gout, apoplexy or epilepsy and that paralysis was unknown—all because of tea. As the French became more familiar with the plant they ceased to think of it as a remedy against all sorts of ailments. Those who had been against it had more and more difficulty maintaining that it was a terrible poison. As the exotic appeal of tea diminished, its use in France receded, and *anglophobic* sentiments were heard. It was said that the English only resorted to drinking tea because they had no wine.

Yet the history of tea in England is far more exciting. The first time a mention of tea appears in English is in the 1669 translation from the Dutch of the book by Jan Nieuhoff, who took part in an expedition to the Chinese court. In this work, a chapter is given over to the 'Roots, Herbs, Flowers, Rice, Trees and Fruits of China'.

In 1600, the British East India Company was founded (and we will refer to it in this book as the East India Company to avoid confusion with the Dutch equivalent). In 1637 the first four English ships appeared in Canton and a foreign settlement was established in Amoy. The Dutch retained their supremacy in trade with the East until around 1650, with the English importing their tea from Holland. At first, the leaf was brought to England as a curiosity but gradually a full trade developed. After the Navigation Act of 1651, only English ships were allowed to transport the tea from Holland and in 1667 tea imports from Holland were banned completely creating a monopoly for the East India Company.

The English consumed their tea and coffee (the latter had become known earlier) in coffee houses, of which the first was opened in Oxford in 1650. This was a direct result of Cromwell's admission of Jews into England—they had been used to such places in Amsterdam. The institution of the coffee house was of tremendous importance in the 17th and 18th centuries with more than 500 of them in London in 1700. Lloyds, the insurance brokers, started off in a coffee house. Thomas Twining, the famous tea firm, started in 1706 with his coffee house in the Strand which, unusually, was also open to ladies. Admission was normally exclusively for gentlemen and many London clubs started life as coffee houses. Thomas Garway's London coffee house, in a 1657 advertisement, ascribed the most incredible qualities to tea and concluded that the leaf possessed such virtues that those nations famous for their longevity, knowledge and wisdom regularly exchanged tea for twice its weight in silver.

"I did send for a cup of tee (a China drink) of which I never had drank before."

On September 20th 1660, Pepys drank his first cup of tea. Catherine of Braganza, the Portuguese wife of Charles II, was an avid tea drinker. Such popularity brought its own penalties. Inevitably, the first tax on tea was introduced—in the form of a levy on the import of the dried leaves, but it made no impact on the now accepted use of tea. More serious were Charles' measures against the coffee houses themselves. The reason for these

measures is quite clear, and was aimed particularly at those houses which had developed into literary clubs, the 'penny universities' so-called because you paid a penny for a cup of tea. These heavily criticised the pro-French politics of the King, and in 1675 Charles II introduced an Act for the Suppression of Coffee Houses which a year later he was forced to withdraw due to public outcry.

In the 18th century the coffee houses began to lose their attraction, with more tea being drunk at home. The tea caddy was kept permanently locked, and the lady of the house always carried the key with her—which gives a clear idea of the price of tea in those days.

The price came down in 1715 when, apart from black Bohea tea (the name comes from the Fukien hill where the tea is grown) green tea began to be imported. As a result the habit spread until it included the rest of the population. This widespread use of tea met with resistance from economists who believed that the lower classes should have better uses for their money, but they forgot the positive aspect of this development, namely that tea replaced beer to a large extent and that water for the tea-pot had to be boiled, which improved hygiene. John Wesley, the Methodist preacher, objected to both tea and alcohol (although Joshua Wedgewood made him a beautiful teapot). There were other moralists who warned that tea corrupted morals and preached against the seductions of the tea gardens. (There was probably more danger to tea blenders; girls who were in service to aristocrats and whose tasks were not always limited to taking care of the master's tea!)

Chinese glass painting (1820) showing foreign settlements.

In 1710 Alexander Pope wrote a rather savage poem dedicated to Queen Anne:

Here thou, great Anna, whom two realms obey
Dost sometimes council take, and sometimes tea.

Apart from the suggestion that Anne took too much advice from different people at the Court, the poem also reveals that the English word 'tea' was still pronounced as the Dutch 'thee'. It is interesting to note that this pronunciation 'thee' originates from the dialect of Amoy where it sounded like 'taj', whereas in pure Cantonese it was pronounced as 'tsja'. In Europe we see that those countries which obtained their tea by sea routes have adopted the Amoy pronunciation whilst in the places where caravans brought the tea overland (Russia and Turkey) the word is 'tchai'. The demarcation line with, for instance, the Czech 'te', runs right across the Slav languages. (Portugal is a special case, the tea was shipped from Canton and so the correct Cantonese word 'chai' is used.)

Acceptance of tea in Scotland was rather reluctant. A dissertation by Dr Thomas Short *Discourses upon Tea* (see quotations) caused panic. He listed the various dangers associated with tea, but his paper led to scores of arguments. Scottish vestries accepted motions prohibiting the

Dr Johnson

use of tea, and the farmers of Fullerton in Ayrshire proclaimed: "if you look at the weakened constitution of the upper classes who drink this strange concoction then we have no need for it but anyone who can afford to be weak, indolent and useless has our blessing".

In England, a last attack was delivered in 1756 by Jonas Hanway, a rather eccentric man who came to the defence of child chimney sweeps and who was the first to protect himself against the rain with an umbrella. In his publication entitled *Essay on Tea*, he said that it was pernicious to health,

impeded diligence and impoverished the nation. One person truly upset by this was Dr Johnson. Johnson, whose kettle hardly had time to cool down, livened up his evenings with tea, sought comfort in tea at midnight and greeted the morning with the same drink, soon settled Hanway's arguments (although they agreed on the point that tea is not really suitable for the lower classes).

Two less palatable aspects of the tea trade in England at this time were the smuggling which had become so extensive that (according to recent calculations) at one period two-thirds of all tea

AN OPINION frequently expressed and certainly gaining ground, is that TEA is gradually deteriorating in quality, that it is not so STRONG and full in flavor, and that it is wanting in the brisk pungent roughness agreeable to the PALATE.

A REASON for this opinion may be found in the IMMENSE QUANTITY of weak, insipid and flavorless TEA imported into this COUNTRY.

THIS inferior Tea will fall into the hands of those dealers who lack KNOWLEDGE OF THE ARTICLE, or the patience necessary to make a right SELECTION.

WITH the numberless packages of inferior and medium quality Tea imported this season, there are some VERY CHOICE TEAS, which for strength and flavor have seldom been equalled in former years,   will supply BLACK TEA of this class at 3/4 per lb., a VERY STRONG, RICH TEA at 2/8 per lb., and a good useful PEKOE FLAVORED TEA at 2/- per lb.

ROBINSONS BRISTOL.

448

consumed must have been illegal, and secondly, the gross adulteration of tea. In 1680 the British customs suggested an import duty of 25 pence per pound of tea irrespective of the value of the tea. This brought the price of the cheapest tea to 35 pence per pound at a time when farm workers earned 40 pence per week.

In Europe, low quality tea was available for less than 5 pence per pound. The smuggling of tea across the North Sea and the Channel soon escalated. Dutch cutters brought the contraband to the English coast where, nightly, small vessels appeared to bring the load ashore. There the tea was hidden in the most unlikely places, with many a verger becoming implicated. One good story tells of the horses which were loaded up and which then followed a mare who knew exactly where the tea was supposed to go. Tea smuggling was such a lucrative pastime that it caused a shortage of farm workers in Kent and, because of its exemption from taxes the Isle of Man profited enormously. Until William Pitt the Younger abolished the tax on tea in 1784, 7,000,000 lbs of tea a year had been smuggled into the country compared with five and a half million which had come in legally. Pitt also announced an amnesty for the smugglers who had generally enjoyed great popularity.

The adulteration of tea resulted in the felling of large numbers of ash trees; blackthorn also provided many 'tea leaves'. Gunpowder and sawdust were mixed in with the green tea. A law of 1777 threatened a fine of £5 or twelve months imprisonment for every pound which had been cut. There is an amusing story about an old tramp who was picking weeds on the outskirts of Brussels and who, when asked exactly what he was doing, answered that he was picking 'tea for the English'.

An impression of the size of the tea trade in Britain in the 18th century can be obtained from the fact that, in 1785, 30,000 wholesalers and retailers were registered as tea merchants. Tea was either consumed at home or in tea gardens situated on the outskirts of the cities. The whole family could go, and relatively little distinction was made between the social classes. The most famous was at Vauxhall, where there was a garden with lanes, shrubs, flowerbeds, ponds, fountains and statues. There were arbours covered with honeysuckle and dog-rose for the tea drinkers to enjoy. Concerts were held in the open air, and when the weather turned bad visitors retreated to the rotunda. The fact that tea was not only drunk by decent, law-abiding citizens becomes apparent from a law dated 1752 which required the tea gardens to be licensed. The extensive spread of London in the 19th century meant the end for most of the tea gardens.

Around 1660 the first tea reached America having been shipped from Holland to New Amsterdam. The well-to-do ladies there drank the tea with sugar and peach leaves. When the English took over the city, and it was renamed New York, tea remained the favourite drink. Special pumps were situated in various places for the most delicious tea water and New York had its Vauxhall tea gardens, too.

The fact that the United States is now a nation of coffee drinkers rather than tea drinkers has to do with the way the tea arrived in America. The East India Company brought the tea from China to England where it paid an import duty to the Crown. The tea was then auctioned by the Company and sold to English merchants, who in turn shipped the tea to America. There it was sold to American merchants who had to be licensed. The colonial authorities imposed a considerable levy on tea and although, in objective terms, the taxes in the American colonies weren't very high, it created a sense of economic submission to the mother country. The taxes flowed without parliamentary or local political control directly into the Treasury. Because the tax on good tea from the East India Company was so high, inferior tea from Holland was also smuggled into America on a massive scale. In 1770, the British Government repealed the hated Towshend Act of Trade and Revenue but, wishing to show its power in America, maintained one of the taxes. This was the tax on tea, which demanded a futile levy of 3 pence per pound (by this time the taxation on tea had become almost entirely a matter of prestige).

The Americans started to drink Dutch tea exclusively thereby driving the East India Company to desperation. In 1773, they managed to get permission to transport the tea directly to the colonies; this was an excellent tea with a low levy on distribution through its own agents. The British exporters, as well as the American tea merchants, were furious, and from that moment the battle really began. The Americans started to boycott tea, and the effect was such that the beverage has never really recovered its popularity to this day and coffee has triumphed. The propaganda against the East India Company as an instrument of imperialism seems melodramatic now, but it was real enough. The end finally came in Boston when, in November 1773, public opinion was running very high against tea and all connected with it. In Philadelphia, the pilot bringing the tea ships into port was threatened with tar and feathers. On 28th November the *Dartmouth* entered Boston harbour with a cargo of tea, and its master, Captain Rotch, was neither allowed to leave the harbour nor to discharge his load. A meeting of the local Parish

council attended by the Governor was invaded by a group of Americans dressed up as Indians. Tempers became frayed, and the Americans marched to the quay where 90 of them, still dressed as Indians, forced their way onto the *Dartmouth* and hurled the tea overboard—342 cases were disposed of in three hours. The date was the 16th December 1773 and the incident is now known as the Boston Tea Party.

In other ports tea was also seized. It took some time for the news to reach England: Benjamin Franklin, who was there at the time, feared for the image of the colonies in Europe. However public opinion in England was little affected. J. M. Scott, who has read all the reports in the English papers of those days, comes to the conclusion that the English government itself was blamed for the event.

After the Boston Tea Party the Government in London passed the Boston Port Bill which closed its harbour, thereby ruining the trade. The arrival of troops in America aroused large-scale resistance and the ensuing war gave birth to the United States.

In Britain, the East India Company, in which many Members of Parliament had vested interests was held responsible for the loss of the Empire in the west. The bad publicity meant the beginning of the end for the Company which, until that time, had had a successful and distinguished history. In 1664 they had opened their own offices in Portuguese Macao. In 1684 a foreign settlement was set up near Canton and in the following year, another settlement was established in Amoy. In 1715, British ships were moored on the quay of Canton and, in 1771, they acquired the right to establish an office on shore for part of the year. In England they held a monopoly, although some enterprising British freighters operated under a foreign flag. The competition from the Dutch, the Portuguese, the Oostende Company (operating on behalf of the Austrian government) and, after 1784 the Americans, posed no serious threat. In 1766, the English ships carried 6,000,000 lbs of tea, the Dutch 4,500,000 lbs and the others 3,000,000 lbs. In the early 19th century the Company faced a setback when Napoleon cut off trade with the Continent, whilst English resistance was growing against the Company's monopoly. Yet they were still making enormous profits in China from the

The 90 Americans, dressed as Indians, assault the Dartmouth and throw the tea overboard.

opium trade. In the first half of the 18th century the dirty job of transporting opium to China had been handled by the Portuguese. The East India Company took over towards the end of that century, mainly because for a long time the Company had experienced problems in finding goods which could be sold in China to pay for the tea and other Chinese products purchased there. Now, finally, the adverse balance could be reduced by exports of opium from India. In 1800, use of opium was prohibited throughout China by an imperial edict. So the East India Company was forced to refrain from actually transporting the drug. Instead, they auctioned the opium in Calcutta and whatever happened to it afterwards was no concern of theirs. Private ships brought it from Bengal to the China Sea and sold it over the side to small boats floating around the isle of Lintin in the Canton river, the buyers bribing the local officials to turn a blind eye to the traffic. Apart from those Chinese who profited directly from the trade, another group of Chinese was heavily dependent: the growing band of addicts. In 1835 their number in China was estimated at two million.

In the West there were powerful national interests behind the drug trade, not all of them British. Though some American firms declined on principle to handle opium, others behaved less ethically. American ships smuggled small quantities of opium from Turkey and Persia, but most of their loads came from India, where the trade was supervised by the East India Company. So you can hardly blame the Chinese for holding Britain responsible. Unfortunately, there was no official British representative in Canton. The foreigners there had no support or protection for their interests from diplomatic or consular representatives of their own nations, and their only means of appeal to the Chinese authorities for redress or grievances was by way of humble petitions presented through the Co-hong, an association of Chinese merchants officially licensed to trade.

In 1834, the British cabinet appointed Lord Napier as Chief Superintendent of Trade. Unfortunately Napier had no experience as a businessman and, what is more important, he was not blessed with imagination or tact; he might have bullied the Chinese, but he was not the man to outwit them.

Napier contravened Chinese regulations by residing in Canton. He was not a merchant, but an official, and he happened to arrive at midsummer when the tea season was over.

The Chinese government now threatened to close the harbour if the opium trade continued. Pressure was mounting, since addiction in China had spread to the upper classes, and more and more silver was leaving the country to pay for it. Lord Napier, misreading the situation, thought that what the subjects of the Emperor themselves wanted was free trade. He posted announcements all over Canton denouncing the Emperor's politics. He also became very upset with Viceroy Lu, who had called him a barbarian. (Tall, bony, red-haired, carrot-faced Napier was the very stereotype of a barbarian to the Chinese.) Lord Napier had to leave Canton and went to Macao, where he died soon afterwards. His successor Elliott was not really better suited for the job. In 1838 the Emperor appointed an imperial high commissioner, Lin Tse-hsü, to deal with the matter. Lin proclaimed a trade embargo, thus forcing on Elliott some degree of cooperation: only after the opium stocks were given up would he lift the siege of the factory in Canton, so that the year's tea crop could

be moved. Elliott told British subjects to surrender their opium, personally guaranteeing that they would be indemnified later. Twenty thousand chests were thus destroyed. The Chinese, well aware that destruction of one year's harvest only meant that the opium would double in value the following year, were adamant that the opium trade should stop forever. Matters were even more complicated by Elliott's promise of indemnity, which put the British government in debt to the tune of over £2,000,000. The big opium houses had far too many connections in London for the government to break its promise. On the other hand, there would be an outcry if the nation learnt of any proposal to compensate the opium merchants with a mere two million of public money. So war was rapidly becoming inevitable. In the absence of any direct contacts with Chinese officialdom the tendency was for disputes to lead to armed clashes, especially as the Britsh, who were the principal Western trading nation in the China Sea, were also by this time the masters of India, and did not find it easy to make the transition from imperial grandeur in Calcutta to downtrodden humility in Canton. On the 5th September 1839 the Opium War broke out, ending with the treaty which declared Hong Kong a British territory.

The tea clippers

The ships that brought the tea from China to
England in the 17th and 18th centuries may have
been fairly modest in size but ranked amongst the
best-equipped trading vessels. The crews were also
much better disciplined than those of other ships.
The most famous tea ships, however, were the
notorious 'tea clippers'. In a way, tea was
instrumental to the development of the yacht
because the smugglers along the British coasts
needed the fastest possible ships when chased by
customs boats. Similarly the Americans needed
fast ships for the dangerous opium trade with
China. The Baltimore clipper was used and proved
to be a success. (The word is derived from the
slang word 'clip' which means 'fast.') These
clippers were too small for the tea trade, and in
1845 a purpose-built ship, the *Rainbow,* with a
capacity of 750 tons, was launched in New York.
Pessimists declared that the *Rainbow* was bound
to sink in the typhoon-stricken waters of the China
Sea. Nothing could have been further from the
truth, and the maiden voyage was a triumph. The
clipper left New York in February and returned in
September. On this her first journey, she had more
than paid for herself.

A very fast clipper was the American-built
Lightning, which on one occasion completed 436
sea miles in 24 hours, an average speed of 18
knots and an all-time record for a sailing ship.

In 1849, the British navigation laws had been
repealed. Feverishly, the British started to build
clippers themselves and ordered the *Lightning*
from the United States. The most famous of the
clipper races, won by those who could bring the
first Chinese tea to auction in Mincing Lane, was
in 1866 between the *Ariel,* the *Taeping* and
Serica. When the ships arrived at Ramsgate, and
had to wait there for a favourable wind to enter the
Thames, great excitement gripped the whole city.
At night, if the wind seemed to be changing
direction, the tea buyer was immediately roused,
quite often for nothing.

During her working life the famous tea clipper
Cutty Sark was plagued by misfortune. In
1872 she hit a flying storm in the Indian Ocean
and was out of the running for the race that year.
Now, however, the *Cutty Sark* is the only
remaining China clipper and is preserved at
Greenwich in a dry dock.

Sadly, the opening of the Suez Canal meant the
end for the tea clippers, and they worked out their
remaining days transporting wool from Australia.

Assam was a desolate area along the Brahmaputra, where in the 19th century Ahamis and
Burmese were at war with each other. A Scottish
major, Robert Bruce, acted as a mercenary for
both parties in turn, but he figures in this book on
tea for quite another reason. In 1823 he discovered
that the inhabitants of Assam made tea from the
leaves of an indigenous tea plant which was a
different variety from the *Camellia Sinensis.* (It is
now generally assumed that the tea plant found its
way from Assam into China.) Robert told his
brother Charles, who sailed the Brahmaputra with
a gun boat, about his discovery. Charles arranged
for some of these plants from Assam to be planted
in the botanical gardens of Calcutta. As long as the
East India Company had the monopoly in the tea
trade with China there was no chance of tea
cultivation in Assam or India. With the end of the
monopoly in 1835 the situation changed. The
isolated and inaccessible district of Assam was
rapidly brought under British control. European
planters and labourers brought in from China died

like flies in Assam's unfavourable climate and Indian tea production did not become profitable until 1852. It was claimed that the poor peasants would benefit, but this was obviously untrue. In fact, vast European-owned plantations were developed which used mainly Chinese labour.

The Dutch however, were more interested in acquiring Chinese tea than Assam along with information on its cultivation in China. The adventurer J.I.L.L. Jacobson, a merchant from Rotterdam (1799–1849), managed to penetrate the interior of Honan in China and observed the cultivation of tea in that area; or so he says in his *Handbook for the Cultivation and Fabrication of Tea* of 1843. (Some consider his stories to be on a par with those of Baron von Munchausen.) In

The Tea clipper Taeping

1829, he came home with a collection of tea plants and 12 Chinese labourers from Fukien. Unfortunately, these labourers were murdered, and Jacobson returned to China with a considerable price on his head. The mandarins captured his interpreter but our hero managed to escape.

In Ceylon between 1869 and 1878 *hemileia vastatrix,* caused the complete destruction of all coffee plants. A few brave planters changed to tea and the result is well-known. The first tea to be planted outside Asia was in 1878 in Nyasaland, now Malawi.

Meanwhile, tea drinking habits in England had changed yet again. In the beginning of the 19th century we saw the arrival of 'low tea' and 'high tea'. Low tea originated in upper class families, comprising a light and expensive snack of cakes and easily-digested sandwiches which filled a gap until dinner was served at eight or nine o clock in the evening. High tea was invented by the middle classes. You would eat one good solid meal at midday, and when you came in from work there would be tea with any leftovers from lunch: cold meat, salads, cheese. In 1894, J. Lyons started his teashops, which provided a service for the ever growing army of office personnel. Gladstone, the Victorian Prime Minister, was an ardent tea drinker. At night he would fill his hotwater bottle with tea so he could warm his feet with his favourite beverage.

> If you are cold, tea will warm you;
> if you are too heated, it will cool you;
> if you are depressed, it will cheer you;
> if you are excited, it will calm you.
>
> *Gladstone* 1865

Tea Drinking in China, Tibet and Japan

Anyone who tries to pin down the origin of tea drinking in China enters an historical maze where little is certain and where much should be regarded as pure fantasy. The mythical Shen Nung is alleged to have been the first to have worked the land and to have known all plants and herbs. He was also believed by historians of the later Han period (25-221 AD) to be the author of the medical book, the *Pen t'sao*. However, many of Shen's plants, tea included, were unknown until the Han era. This discrepancy arose because the early scholars assumed that knowledge existing in their time had existed for ever; it was also considered quite acceptable to use events from ancient history as precedents for the politics of their own days. As there was no united Chinese empire until 221 BC, the idea of Shen Nung as emperor of one united China in 2750 BC is completely absurd.

As far as the *Pen t'sao* is concerned the form in which we know it dates from the third century AD. It mentions 'bitter tasting t'u from the hills of Ichow,' which was supposed to be good for any swelling or abcesses in the head and 'would diminish the desire for sleep'. Here a new problem arises: What is *t'u?* The problem stems from the Chinese script where there are no phonetic signs to establish the pronunciation, only ideograms and symbols. The Chinese sign for tea (see example a) was not used until the 7th century. It is derived from the symbol (see example b) for a different plant, the thistle, *t'u*. Before the seventh century, this sign was also used for tea so we can never be certain if it refers to thistles or tea! This makes the *Shih Ching,* the Book of Odes of Confucius (about 500 BC), an unreliable source when it asks 'Who say that the t'u is bitter? It is as sweet as the tsi.' (shepherd's purse).

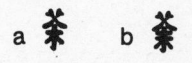

Buddhist sources give us more information than Confucius. A legend tells of the Chinese scholar, Gan Lu, who visited India where he was converted to Buddhism, returning with this new religion along with tea seeds. The legend seems to contain an element of truth. There are indications that the introduction of Buddhism into China *did* coincide with the origin of the tea drinking habit. In the 19th century the tea plant was found growing wild in Assam, and it is likely that *camellia sinensis* grew wild in a rather larger area including Assam, Burma and Yun-Nan and Szechuan in South West

tea and fill the bowls. He has to buy the tea on the market in Wu-Yang (in Szechuan).

The authenticity of the following story is also beyond doubt. It comes from *The History of the Three Kingdoms* and was written around 270AD. In 264, King Sun Hao, a dissolute man famous for his drunkenness, was on the throne. At his orgies every guest had to drink seven sheng of wine. His favourite, Wei Chao, just couldn't manage this—three sheng was his limit. So a friend secretly gave him tea instead of wine, and the discovery of this deception meant the downfall of the poor Wei Chao who was incarcerated in a dungeon and executed in 273.

China). Tea drinking and Buddhism would have reached China from Burma via Annam (the north of Vietnam). The first tea on Chinese soil was grown in Szechuan.

Because of this, many historians consider a mention of tea in the first century BC to be authentic. The surviving poem 'Tung yuch' (the contract for the slaves) by Wang Pao from Szechuan, Poet Laureat to Emperor Hsuan, mentions a date corresponding to February 18 59BC. In this poem Wang Pao visits a widow with a disobedient slave and takes over this slave as his own. All the slave's tasks are written into a contract. When a dinner is held he has to boil the

The author, Chang Hua (232-300) described the suspicion with which the new beverage was regarded in the north. In a passage entitled 'Food to be avoided', he says that the drinking of real tea would cause people to suffer from insomnia.

Gradually tea was drunk less for its medicinal effect and more for its taste. The habit became increasingly accepted in the turbulent times following the Han period. We find a definition of tea in Kuo P'o's adaptation of the dictionary, the

Erh Ya which was produced about this time. The Emperor Wu Ti (483-493) was a great lover of tea, and after his death gifts of tea had to be made to him. Under the Sui (589-617) and the T'ang (618-907) dynasties, China once again developed a powerful central authority, and from the taxes raised on tea after 793, it is clear that it had become a valuable commodity. Po Min-Chung, the Prime Minister from 846, was nicknamed 'the tea boy'.

Lu Yu, patron saint of the tea merchants and author of the *Ch'a Ching* or 'Ode to Tea' was a foundling raised by a Buddhist priest. He refused to become a priest himself and ran away. He joined a circus and subsequently dedicated himself to science. Thanks to his reputation as the greatest tea expert of his day, he was commissioned by the tea merchants to write the *Ch'a Ching* (780). This classic work was an instant success; so overwhelming that Lu Yu chose the existence he had tried to escape in his youth. He retreated as a hermit into the mountains.

All sorts of information is given about tea in his book. In the 19th century it was a source of knowledge for people like Fortune and Jacobson who tried to purloin the secret of tea cultivation from the Chinese. Lu Yu also stood at the cradle of the Japanese tea ceremony. To him, tea drinking was obviously an art.

He said that the tea expert was a scientist and should be respected as such. According to him, the true tea expert should be guided only by the taste; colour being no indication of quality. His writing is full of rich metaphors, often derived from agriculture, and reflecting the rural society in which he lived. Here are three brief quotes from the book:

'Tea leaves come in a thousand different shapes some look like the boots of a Tartar, some like the breast of a buffalo, some like clouds approaching from the mountains, some look like the rippling of the water caused by breeze, some have a dull brown colour and look like freshly ploughed soil covered with puddles after a heavy rainfall. All these are good teas.'

'Winged creatures fly, fur-covered creatures run, creatures with a throat talk. These three types live in the space between heaven and earth. They eat and drink to live, but whilst drinking, how far removed they are from understanding! To quench thirst drink soup, to drive out sadness drink wine, to acquire blissful sleep drink tea.'

'When the water boils for the first time, something akin to the eyes of the fish appear on the surface and a faint sound can be heard. Then the gurgling of a brook develops with a string of pearls round the edge: this is the second boiling. Then the turbulent waves appear: this is the third boiling.'

Lu Yu considered the blue glazing of the north to have been ideal for the teapot because it enhanced the green colour of the drink even further, whilst in a white cup the tea would appear pink and tasteless. In the T'ang period only cake tea was known: the leaves were steamed, pressed into a mould and baked into a cake, then boiled in an earthenware pot with boiling water whilst rice, ginger, salt, orange peel, cloves, milk and sometimes onions were added. In Tibet, a similar drink is still prepared today with yak butter and called *tsampa*. According to some, the Russian way of adding lemon to tea also stems from the customs of the T'ang period.

The reign of Sung (960–1127) is sometimes called the romantic era of Chinese culture, and during this time whisked tea replaced the cake tea. The tea leaves were ground to a powder which was then whisked in hot water with a bamboo whisk. Salt and cloves were no longer added. These changes affected the choice of the tea service, and small, rather heavy, bowls were used, coloured blue, black or dark brown.

An emperor who shouldn't be overlooked is Hui Tsung (1101–1124). He was more dedicated to art and science than to politics, and was a great tea expert. He wrote a dissertation on the twenty different kinds of tea proclaiming that white tea was the rarest and of the highest quality.

At the court, tea drinking was a ritual of great elegance and refinement. Special competitions were arranged in which tea experts had to recognise the different kinds. In the big cities there were tea houses. Poets sung the praises of tea and one such poet, Wang Yuan Chih, praised tea because 'her delicate bitterness reminded him of the taste left by good advice'. In the meantime, the area where tea was grown had spread enormously. It had advanced up the valley of the Yang-tse-kiang and reached Fukien under the Sung dynasty, which by now was producing an excellent tea. Lu Yu was worshipped as a kind of patron saint of the tea trade, with the potters of Kung-hsien (in Honan) making small figurines of him. Anyone who bought ten pots got one free.

Tea drinking became common practice amongst the middle and working classes through the Ch'an of Zen Buddhists, who also cultivated the tea ceremony in Japan. Zen is derived from the Sanskrit word *Dhyana,* or meditation. Although a Buddhist sect, many of its principles are taken from Taoism which strongly emphasises the seeking of beauty here in the world. According to Zen Buddhism, one can realise oneself through concentrated meditation, since it is one of the six ways to reach the state of Buddha.

A clue as to the age of the tea ceremony can be found with Po-Chang (720–814), a pupil of the Zen monk, Ma-tsu, who gave instructions on the drinking of tea in monastries. Special monks (*ch'a-t'ou*) offered tea to the spirit of Bodhidharma and served the other monks at table.

Why is it that the formal drinking of tea

THE Civilizing Influence of TEA.

Tea IS SUGGESTIVE OF A THOUSAND WANTS, FROM WHICH SPRING THE DECENCIES AND LUXURIES OF SOCIETY. THE SAVAGE MAY DRINK WATER OUT OF HIS CALABASH TILL DOOMSDAY; BUT GIVE HIM TEA, AND HE STRAIGHTWAY EXERCISES HIS FACULTIES IN THE INVENTION OF A CUP WORTHY OF SUCH A BEVERAGE

IS IT GOING TOO FAR TO INQUIRE WHETHER TEA MAY NOT HAVE BORNE AN IMPORTANT PART IN THE FORMATION OF THAT GENTLENESS AND TRACTABILITY OF CHARACTER, WHICH KEEPS THE CHINESE CALM AND ORDERLY, EVEN IN THE MIDST OF POLITICAL REVOLUTIONS?

REGISTERED DESIGN 606

ROBINSONS BRISTOL.

(expressing a certain outlook on life called 'teaism') and the tea ceremony, are important in Japan whilst they have disappeared in China although tea is still drunk in great quantities there? One reason was the intrusion of nomadic tribes into China from the north. Firstly, the Kin nomads controlled northern China, then later the Mongolians established their reign in China. Marco Polo failed to mention tea when he stayed at the court of Kubla Khan from 1271 to 1294 because tea was not drunk at his court. Even though he saw himself as a great man, Kubla Khan was regarded as a barbarian by the Chinese intellectual elite and they all retreated to the South, far from the court.

The Ming Dynasty (1368–1644) brought a period of restoration, but the old, refined, court culture never returned. Tea drinking was now universally practised by all classes of the population, but the upper classes still distinguished themselves by their appreciation of high quality expensive tea, carefully prepared. Etiquette dictated that guests should be offered exquisite tea, and the act of drinking tea became a social ceremony. The tea was brewed by pouring boiling water over the leaves—the manner of preparation adopted by Western Europe in the 17th century. Light, white porcelain was particularly favoured for drinking.

A very interesting story is the bartering of tea for horses which developed during the Ming era. As early as the beginning of our first century AD the Chinese were aware that the horses from the north were better than their own. Special expeditions were organised just to acquire them. The Mongolian empire was founded entirely on the possession of horses and this fact taught the Mings that horses were essential for a strong China. The breeding of horses was not very successful, partly because of the lack of suitable pasture land in China and so

the Emperors sent trade missions to the non-Chinese nations of central Asia resulting in an agreement to purchase horses. There was, however, the problem of payment since both silk and silver were too valuable. The exchange of horses for tea proved to be the most satisfactory as the people in the cold north-west badly needed the tea. Despite their official disdain for trade in general, the Chinese on their side realised the importance of this special trade. Under a government decree merchants were allowed, indeed encouraged, to trade for horses, and because of the existence of the tea monopoly, merchants who exported tea privately were threatened with heavy penalties. However, the supervising civil servants were so badly paid that they actively smuggled tea themselves.

We have the figures for the year 1389, when a first-class horse was worth 120 chin of tea (one chin is equal to 586.82 grms or about 1¼ lbs). The average horse reached 70 chin and a poor one would fetch 50 chin of tea with about 1,000,000 chin being paid for 15,000 horses. Due to the unrest developing in the north-west the army gradually became unable to transport the tea from

Szechuan to Shensi in the north-west. This meant that the importing of horses often came to a halt, even though the demand for them was greater than ever. A solution seemed to lie in planting tea in Shensi province. However, in times of famine, the population of Shensi exchanged its tea for grain from central China. To help maintain the trade the tea monopoly was lifted, and replaced by an obligation for the tea merchants to supply 40% of their tea to the state. This they did but the 40% proved to be inferior to the rest of their tea. So the state got the worst part.

Corruption and weak central authority as well as the fact that horses were now needed more in the north east of China led to the disappearance of the tea for horse trade and tea began to find its way via Canton to Europe.

In the 9th century the first tea was imported into Tibet from China where it is still prepared in the same way as it was in the Chinese T'ang period. A piece of tea cake is broken up, mixed with water and various ingredients and cooked into a thick stew. The Tibetan speciality is the added yak butter. There, on the roof of the world, gallons of tea are consumed, for the climate induces a great thirst and the butter satisfies the need for fat. Until the 1950's, tea briquettes were used in Tibet as currency, just as they had been centuries ago in isolated corners of the Chinese empire. In some areas they were valued more highly even than silver. There is an amusing story about the French missionaries Père Huc and Père Gabet who went to the Himalayas in 1846. They came across a great tea party held by pilgrims for 4,000 lamas and recounted how, in this sanctury, the priests modestly hid their worldly wooden tea bowls in the folds of their habits. (For those interested in the novelty of preparing tea the Tibetan way I am pleased to say that tea briquettes or tea cakes are available through specialist shops).

Japan, the country where the ritual of the tea ceremony symbolises a whole philosophy of life (teaism), obviously needs discussion. For those who want to go more deeply into the subject there are some titles listed in the back of this book. The most concise—and definitely the most charming—is Kakuzo Okakura's *The Book of Tea*, a true gem, which tries to familiarise Western audiences with Japanese aesthetics by exploring in depth the essence of the tea ceremony. Okakura, who died in 1913, was for a long time curator of the Department of Oriental Art at the Boston Museum of Fine Arts.

The oldest story about tea in Japan concerns Emperor Shomu who gave tea to one hundred Buddhist monks at the Imperial Court. In 801 the monk Saicho, later renamed Dengyo Daishi, brought some tea seeds from China to be planted in Yeisan. Gradually tea drinking became generally accepted. The whisked Sung powder tea reached Japan in 1191 thanks to Eisai Zenji, who had studied the Zen school of philosophy on the continent. His tea was planted in the Uji district near Kyoto, which still produces the best quality (green) tea. The Japanese legend about the origin of tea can be found on the back of this book. The monk Bodhidharma (his Japanese name is Daruma) came to Canton from India in 520 AD. His last years were spent meditating in a rock temple near Nanking. Despite the fact that Bodhidharma never visited Japan, he is a prominent figure in Japanese visual art. In the Middle Ages in Japan, tea was mostly drunk by the monks of the Zen sect, although the habit became more and more accepted by the upper classes. The Chinese habit of organising tea competitions (*tocha's*) was adopted in the 14th century. The guests were presented with various different sorts of tea which had to be recognised. In 1338 these competitions were banned because they were used as a cover up for gambling and debauchery.

Japanese customs were not interrupted by Mongolian invasions as they had been in China and they were able to develop freely. The tocha and the teaism of the Zen priest came together as the *Chanoyu* or Tea Ceremony. Cha-no-yu literally means 'hot water tea'. To explain something about the philosophy of the tea ceremony without making the typically European mistake of writing about the 'inscrutable' and 'mysterious' Japanese whose thinking is so 'differ-

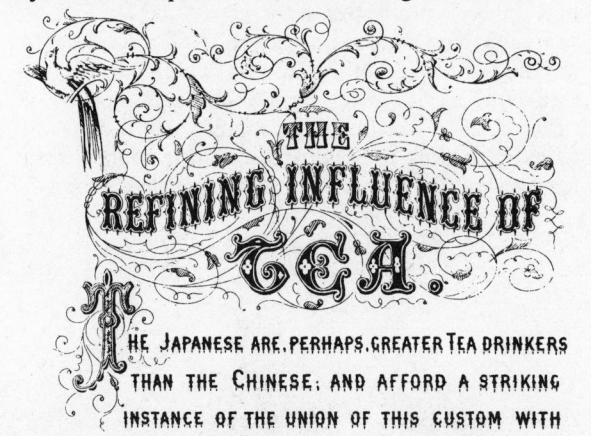

THE REFINING INFLUENCE OF TEA.

THE JAPANESE ARE, PERHAPS, GREATER TEA DRINKERS THAN THE CHINESE; AND AFFORD A STRIKING INSTANCE OF THE UNION OF THIS CUSTOM WITH A HIGH STATE OF REFINEMENT AND POLITENESS.

EVERY INDIVIDUAL IN JAPAN IS TAUGHT READING, WRITING, AND THE HISTORY OF HIS OWN COUNTRY. MORNING CALLS AND DINNERS ARE AS COMMON AS IN EUROPE, BUT MORE ESPECIALLY GRAND TEA MEETINGS AT WHICH THE MATRONS AMUSE THEMSELVES WITH ORNAMENTAL WORK, AND THE OTHERS WITH SINGING AND DANCING.

THERE IS NO COUNTRY IN THE WORLD WHERE TEA LEADS MORE DIRECTLY THAN IN JAPAN TO THE STUDY OF THE COMFORTS AND ELEGANCIES OF SOCIETY. THE EXHIBITION OF PORCELAIN AND LACQUERED WARE IS MAGNIFICENT.

ent', I will mainly use quotations in this chapter. Firstly sayings from various famous Japanese tea masters.

The Zen master Takuan (1573–1645) said 'The tea ceremony is not a complicated ritual nor is it just a superficial performance. Chanoyu means spiritual understanding of a harmonious blend of Heaven and Earth. It is contemplating, around the hearth, the all-encompassing presence of the five elements, whereby mountains, rivers, rocks and trees are found as they are in Nature. It is the drawing of the refreshing water from Nature's well, the awareness in one's own mouth of its very taste. How magnificent is this enjoyment of the harmonious blend of Heaven and Earth.'

The despot Toyotomi Hideyoshi, had somehow grasped something of the teachings of Rikyu (the greatest tea master of all time) when he wrote the following poem:

'When tea is made with water,
drawn from the depths of the spirit,
of which the bottom is unfathomable,
then we have truly realised what is called
cha-no-yu'

From the tea master Nakaro Kazuma (beginning of the 18th century) 'The essence of the Cha-no-yu is to cleanse the six senses of any impurities. By observing the *kakemono* in the *tokonoma* (see page 31) and the flowers in the vase the sense of smell is cleansed; by listening to the boiling of the water in the iron kettle and the dripping of water from the bamboo pipe the ears are cleansed; by tasting the tea the mouth is cleansed; and by handling the tea service the sense of touch is cleansed. When in this manner all the senses have been cleansed the mind itself is purified. The art of the tea is in the first place a mental skill and I strive to follow for every hour of the day the spirit of the tea which is by no means a purely pleasurable occupation.'

The western thinking about Japan is determined by concepts which are essentially contradictory. On one hand militarism and hardness (harakiri!) are attributed to the Japanese character; on the other the Japanese landscape and Japanese art are described in terms of 'harmony' and 'gentleness' (cherry blossom!).

In Japanese the characters for 'harmony' and 'gentleness of spirit' are identical. With the tea ceremony we should keep the latter in mind—the gentleness of spirit. Someone who has little feeling for 'life's beauty' is described as 'having no tea in him' whilst the complete aesthetic sometimes has 'too much tea in him'. Teaism is sometimes called the 'art of concealing beauty so that it can be discovered, the art of implying the unspeakable, the noble secret of self-mockery restrained but still profound, the smile of philosophy'.

Teaism is a cult based on the worship of Beauty. Love for nature and the use of simple materials are essential. It means purity, harmony, reciprocal tolerance. In some ways it glorifies the aristocracy of taste, but at the same time its symbol is 'the cup of humanity'. The original ideal was the creation in a tea room of a Buddhist Land of Purity on earth. *Sabi*, 'tranquility', is essential for the Cha-no-yu. Apart from tranquility, simplicity, frugality and solitude, the word Sabi also implies an 'aesthetic appreciation of poverty'! The concept of pure poverty denotes an indescribable, peaceful joy, and the art of tea should give artistic form to this idea. In a simple, bare tea room we suddenly find something very valuable.

The Samurai, the Japanese fighter, however much he might be occupied with war and battle,

realised that he would not live like this continually, but at certain times would need the opportunity to escape from his everyday existence. Tea satisfied this need, and he retreated briefly into a quiet corner of his subconscious self, symbolised by a tea room no larger than 3 metres square. When he left the room not only did he feel refreshed in mind and body, but the memory of things more lasting and valuable than war and battle had been intensified too.

In 1447 the shogun Yoshimasa had a tea room measuring 3 x 3 metres built at his palace in Kyoto which is the oldest known to us. The greatest tea master of them all, Sen-no Rikyu, (late 16th century), built the first detached tea house. The building consisted of the *sukiya,* which can be best translated as 'the dwelling of the imagination' (although the word suki has many secondary meanings), then the *muzi-ya,* the ante room for the tea service, the *yoritsuki,* the waiting room, and

the *roji,* the path which led to the tea room and broke the connection with the outside world, symbolising the first stage of the meditation. The door is only 3 ft high. Humbly bowing down, the Samurai enters, leaving his sword behind.

Sen-no Rikyu became a high priest in 1586; he purified and institutionalised the tea ceremony but he also organised large-scale tea parties. For instance, in 1588 a tea gathering for 500 guests from all social circles took place in the palatial gardens which covered an area of 3 square miles. From a great distance, the boiling of the water could be heard. In his daily life Rikyu did not refrain from luxury, but in his writing and in the stories which have survived for centuries the emphasis is always on 'sabi', tranquility. The Rules of Rikyu were as follows:

1. As soon as the guests were assembled in the

Tea picking. A Japanese screen which was one of a series of 18 presented to William 111 by the shogun in 1860. Leiden Rijksmuseum voor Volkenkunde.

waiting room they announced themselves by striking a wooden gong.

2.   When entering the ceremony it was important that one should not only have a clean face and clean hands but a clean heart as well.

3.   The host approached his guests in welcome and led them inside. If because of his poverty the host was unable to offer his guests the tea and other essentials for the ceremony, or even if the trees and the rocks did not please a guest, then he could leave immediately. After a light meal, the guests retired.

4.   As soon as the water made a sound like the wind through the pine trees, and the clock chimed, the guests had to return from the waiting room as it would be amiss to forget the right moment for the water and the fire.

5.   It was traditionally forbidden to discuss worldly affairs inside or outside the tea house. This applied to political discussions and especially to gossip. The only permissible subject was the tea and the tea societies.

6.   Neither guest nor host could use flattery during a true, pure tea ceremony whether it be by words or by deeds.

7.   The gathering could last no longer than two Japanese hours, which is the equivalent to four European hours.

These rules of Rikyu were discussed during the gathering. Theoretically, class differences were ignored within the tea society. The rules are still the same today.

Rikyu's end was a sad one. The Taiko was stricken by the beauty of Rikyu's daughter who had recently become a widow. The Taiko demanded her for his mistress, and when Rikyu explained that the lady was still in mourning for her husband and asked to be excused, the Taiko flew into a temper. Whereupon Rikyu was ordered to take his own life. His last tea session in the company of his closest friends was vividly described by Okakura who concluded: 'With a smile on his face Rikyu left for the unknown'.

In the tea room, the tokonoma or alcove is situated. (The altar of the chapel in a Zen monastery was the prototype for the tokonoma.) In the tokonoma hangs a painting or a calligraphy—kakemono. From the post of the altar hangs a bamboo or woven vase in which there are flowers bound by special rules. An azalea or an ipomoea is never used in a tea room. Entering the sukiya on a close summer's day it is delightful to find one single lily, freshly bedewed. The vision of this immediately invigorated the mind.

The water kettle is usually made of iron,

sometimes of bronze. The surface is kept intention-
ally rough and artists attempt to renew the shape of
the kettle continually. The incense burned during
the ceremony should not be too overpowering. The
incense case is often an exquisite piece of art
especially admired by guests. The tea bowl should
be fairly thick so as not to conduct the heat too
much; have a rough outside so that the bowl is
easily held; a rim curved slightly inwards to
prevent spillage; a glaze which is soft and
agreeable to the mouth. Green tea shows up best in
black bowls.

A prosaic westerner might describe the tea of the
Cha-no-yu as 'thick, foamy, lukewarm and green'
and although that may be an accurate statement in
itself, it shows that the essence of the tea ceremony
has escaped him completely. The Japanese guest
knows better. Etiquette demands that he shows
respect for his host by making loud smacking
noises to express his enthusiasm for the taste of the
tea. The same etiquette demands that the host
should apologise for the tea afterwards and say
that it was really very poor.

The tea ceremony which I now want to describe
in more detail is the one from the Ura-Senke
school whose leader Soshitsu Sen, is a fourteenth
generation descendant of Sen Rikyu. The ceremony
includes:

1. The first session during which a light meal (the
kaiseki) is served.
2. The *nakadachi,* when the guests have to
retreat.
3. The *goza-iri,* the true tea ceremony, during
which *koicha,* thick tea is drunk.
4. The drinking of *usucha,* thin tea.

In the first session the host leads the five guests
along the roji to the tea room and on the way they
can wash their hands with fresh water in a stone
basin. After entering the sukiya every guest kneels
in front of the tokonoma in worship. They then
admire the roll on the wall of the tokonoma. The
seating is arranged so that the most important
guest sits closest to the host. Then kaiseki is
served. When the kaiseki is finished the guests
return from the sukiya and wait. The goza-iri is
announced by beating the gong five or seven times
whereupon the guests re-enter. More outside light
is now allowed into the sukiya and the roll on the
wall is replaced by a vase of flowers. These are
admired by the guests—as is the kettle. Now the
host enters with the rest of the tea equipment.
Everything is thoroughly cleaned again and when
this is done the host takes the tea cannister and
spoon and puts *matcha* (three spoonfuls per guest)
in the bowl and pours hot water from the kettle. He
then beats the tea with a bamboo whisk until it
thickens to the consistency of pea soup and puts the
bowl in front of the hearth. The first guest
approaches on his knees and picks up the bowl. He
bows to his fellow guests, takes the bowl in the
palm of his left hand whilst supporting his elbow
with his right hand, takes a sip, praises the taste

and then takes two more sips. He wipes the part of the rim from which he has drunk with kaishi paper and passes the bowl to the second guest and the same ritual is repeated. When the last of the five guests has drunk he offers the bowl to the guest of honour who presents it to the host. The usucha, which is often held separately, is a simplified form of goza-iri.

The words of the great Zen expert, Daisetz Suzuki, are worth reading.

'The ipomoea, which will only last for a few hours on a summer's day, is as meaningful as the pine tree whose gnarled trunk withstands the wintery cold. The microscopic organisms are as valid a manifestation of life as the elephant or the lion—in fact they are more resilient because even if all other forms of life were to disappear from the surface of the earth the microbes would continue their existence. Who then would deny when I drink my tea in my tea room that I imbibe the whole universe, and that the moment when I pick up the tea bowl is eternal beyond time and space. The art of the tea really teaches us much more than the harmony of things and how to protect them from contamination or simply the way of retreat into a state of tranquil contemplation—it teaches us to fight the inner emptiness!'

Finally a quotation from Daito Kokushi of Kyoto:

'If your ears see
and your eyes hear
no doubts will you have
How naturally does the rain
drip from the eaves'

The Cultivation and Processing of Tea

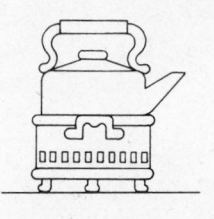

Botanists distinguish the following varieties of tea bushes which are closely related: the *Camellia sinensis* is the Chinese bush which even without pruning keeps the shape of a bush and can reach a maximum height of three to four metres. The bush is sufficiently hardy for the temperate zones (China, Japan) and can tolerate even snow and frost in Georgia. The *Camellia assamica*, without pruning, can develop into a sizeable tree with a height of 15 to 20 metres which is well suited to the tropics! The leaves can be as long as 35 cm. So far, little research has been done on the varieties from the Shan countries (North Burma and North Thailand) which are sometimes called the 'small-leaved Assam' and grow in the wild.

There are several crosses or hybrids of the *sinensis* and the *assamica* which are used extensively. As the name implies, the tea plant belongs to the camellia family. It bears its dark green leathery leaves all the year round and the blossom consists of small pink flowers which resemble jasmine. The fruits resemble nutmeg but are used less and less for propogation. There is now a preference for *vegetative* propogation involving the use of cuttings from a parent plant. This has proved to be exceptionally productive and produces plants resistant to disease. On a Brooke Bond plantation in South India there is a plant which has generated at least three million other tea bushes.

The most important factors influencing the quality of the tea are the climate, the soil conditions—and, of course, the treatment of the growing plant. The tea plant is incredibly tough and the only thing it cannot tolerate at all is wet soil conditions. Trees which provide shade are important, and the volcanic soil reclaimed from tropical forest makes an ideal growing medium. In hilly or mountainous country, terraces are often built to prevent erosion in the plantations. On a typical modern plantation in India, Ceylon or Indonesia the bushes are planted at a distance of 0.7 to 1.4 metres apart and pruned so as to facilitate picking.

After three years (longer for high altitude areas) the plant is ready. First of all, it is cut back completely and subsequent careful pruning will be necessary from time to time.

In tropical areas where the tea can be harvested throughout the year, the tea planter and his assistants fight a running battle against weeds and diseases. There are three types of picking, fine, medium and rough, which are young shoots comprising a leaf bud with two, three or four

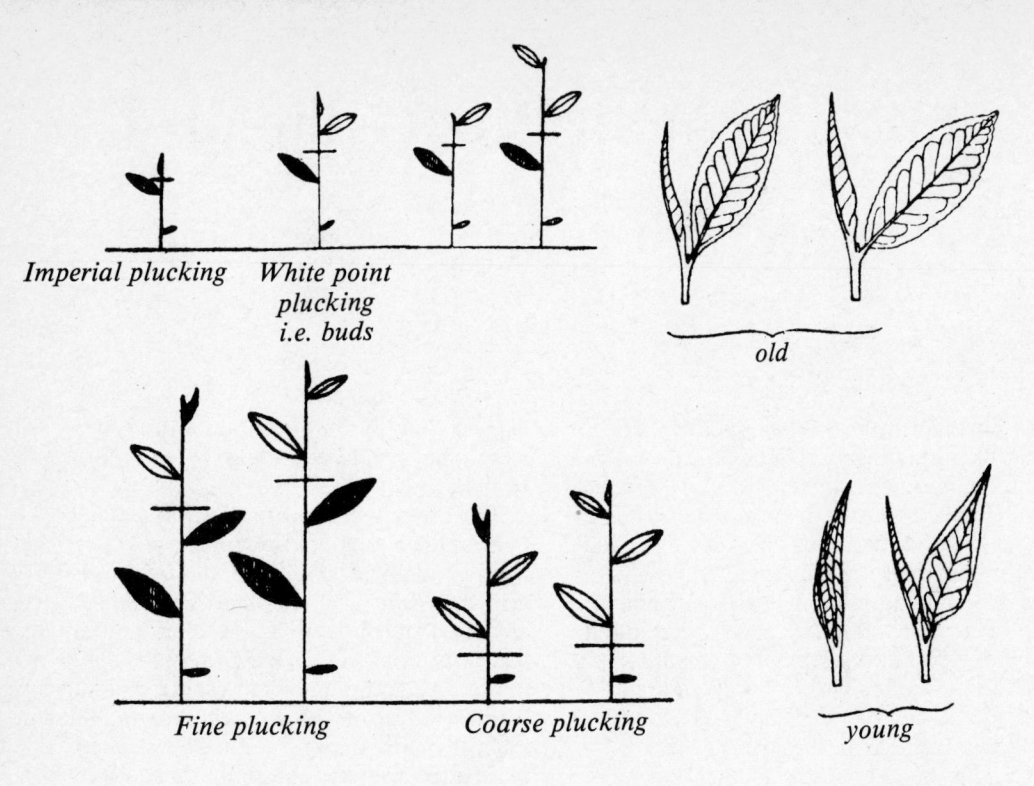

*Imperial plucking   White point
                       plucking
                       i.e. buds*

old

Fine plucking   Coarse plucking

young

leaves respectively. The expression 'two leaves and a bud' may be familiar. The leaf bud is small and still closed, the two leaves are tender, juicy and green. In the lowlands, picking may be carried out every seven days. Higher up, an interval of about ten days is necessary. (Further details of where picking can be carried out all the year round, where it can be done only at certain times of the year, and how the seasons influence the quality of the tea, will be given when we deal with the various countries.) On the plantations, women are most proficient at picking the tea between finger and thumb, and they do this with a combination of accuracy and high speed. Usually they carry large baskets on their backs which are handed in at a central point for processing in the factory, because tea, in contrast to coffee, is processed on the plantation.

We will not concern ourselves here with the laborious traditional methods of the Chinese peasants. The orthodox method of preparation consists of the following processes: withering, curling and wet sorting, fermentation, drying and dry sorting. This all applies to the processing of black tea.

Withering—fresh leaves cannot be curled because they contain too much water and therefore break easily. For this reason the freshly picked leaf is spread out on racks in thin layers. This usually happens in the attic of the tea factory. A flow of warm air (25–30°C) is passed through the area and during this process, which can last from 12 to 18 hours, the leaf loses about 60% of its moisture.

Rolling—or curling, prepares the leaf for fermentation. Rolling breaks open the leaf cells and allows the cell contents to blend. In wet sorting, called roll breaking, the different sized leaf parts are separated as far as possible.

Fermentation—this is not an accurate description of the process, since in actual fact it is oxidation that takes place. In a damp room with a low ventilation rate and a controlled temperature the leaf is spread out in layers 10cm thick. Here the bursting of the leaf cells cease and, in the presence of oxygen, the juices from the leaf react together chemically. In this way the tea forms its special properties.

Drying and Leaf Sorting—When the tea is dried the fermentation stops. This is usually done by heating the tea with hot air at 85–88°C for twenty minutes on a conveyor belt. The leaf which has so far had a copper colour now gets the familiar black appearance. This copper colour reappears in the tea leaves in the tea pot! Through a system of reciprocating sieves the tea is sorted into different leaf grades and packed into plywood tea chests. (1000 kilos of green tea makes about 220 kilos of black tea.)

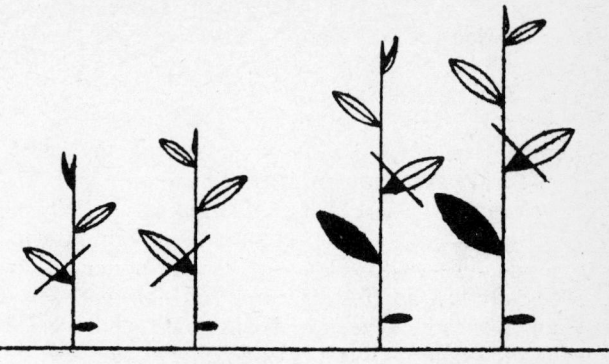

Plucking to maintain the level table

A woman can pick around 35 kilos a day which is the equivalent of 8 kilos of processed tea. On an average plantation in Assam, for example, a daily harvest of from 12 to 15000 kilos of fresh leaves can be expected.

Different methods are used to increase the speed of the orthodox method of processing. The CTC method is often used, especially in Africa and India. CTC stands for (1) crushing (2) tearing (3) curling. After the leaf has been wilted it is curled for 30 minutes and then mangled between the rollers of the CTC machines which rotate at different speeds. One drawback is that this will not produce leaf tea but broken tea. However, with the large scale use of teabags and the demand for quick brew, this method seems to promise the most for the future. A recent development is the use of the Rotorvane for the curling process—this is a cross between a fruit press and a mincer. In the trade, the following grades are distinguished according to leaf-type and grain respectively.

1. Whole leaf tea

Flowery Orange Pekoe (FOP) with Darjeeling also Golden Flowery Orange Pekoe (GFOP) and Tippy Golden Flowery Orange Pekoe (TGFOP): a thin stringy leaf with tip.

Tip is the name given to the golden, silvery or greyish parts of the tea. These are the tips of the young leaves that contain less cell sap and therefore do not darken during fermentation. When making tea, the hot water colours them light brown to golden. Tea with golden tips is very popular, especially in Iran. Tea with tips is a sign that young leaves have been used and that they have been picked carefully; it says nothing about the quality.

Orange Pekoe (OP) is a fancy grading. OP contains no tips and the tops are thin and light.

The leaves are long and stringy; a little larger than the FOP. The percentage may lie around 10%. The name Orange Pekoe only indicates a type of leaf, it says nothing about the quality. The name 'Pekoe' comes from the Chinese 'pak ho', meaning white hair. Orange has nothing to do with oranges or orange blossom. It is most likely derived from the Dutch House of Orange in which case it could have been an indication of top quality.

Pekoe (P) and Flowery Pekoe (FP) are shorter and coarser than the Orange Pekoe, often the leaves are more open, in other words not so tightly rolled. Flowery Pekoe from Sri Lanka (Ceylon) usually has a leaf that is rolled up into a little ball, called 'shotty' or 'curly'. For both P and FP production average is around 1%. The after-taste of FP is stronger than OP, because OP contains more veins and less 'flesh' from the tea leaf. The P is lighter at the top than the BOP and sells well, partly due to its pretty leaf.

Pekoe Souchong (PS) and Souchong (S) are the coarsest of the leaf gradings. Open, broad leaf, thin in consistency when poured out. Souchong is the Chinese name for the coarsest commodity in a consignment destined for the trade.

2. Broken and small-leaved tea

Flowery Broken Orange Pekoe (FBOP), with Darjeeling also Golden Flowery Broken Orange Pekoe (GFBOP) and Tippy Golden Flowery Broken Orange Pekoe (TGFBOP).

The finest and most aromatic of the broken gradings. A carefully finished well-rolled leaf with many golden tips. This tea sells well owing to its attractive appearance and delicate aroma. Its after-taste is stronger than that of similar kinds of leaf. A satisfactory percentage lies around 10%.

Tea Circular

have on hand some rare and choice growths of INDIAN TEA

From the Assam and Darjeeling Company's Estates.

ALSO A LARGE VARIETY OF

Kaisow, Moning, Lapsang Souchong and Flowery Scented Orange Pekoe,

FROM THE MOST NOTED

Chinese Plantings,

Some of which are of rare excellence being the finest growths of the Season and are especially recommended to the notice of Connoisseurs, these are also sold blended together to suit the varied tastes of our Customers, many of whom prefer a combination, but do not care to purchase a number of different kinds in order to mix them themselves. The following mixings from our list are particularly recommended.

THE "ASSAM COMPANY'S" MIXTURE, 2/

„ "DARJEELING,"   Dº   2/6

The London Tea Auction.

Broken Orange Pekoe (BOP) is a well-finished leaf containing slightly less tip. Stronger in the top than the FBOP albeit not as aromatic. This grading accounts for about 50% of the tea produced but percentages between 60-70% are not uncommon. The sale of BOP (and thus its value) is determined by quality and outward appearance of the black leaf. On some Indian plantations FBOP is called Broken Orange Pekoe (BOP); in Sri Lanka (Ceylon), however, it is a semi-leaf tea, a grading that lies between the Pekoe and BOP.

Broken Pekoe (BP) is of the same dimensions as BOP, sometimes slightly more robust. It can be easily recognized by the form of the cuttings. It contains no tip and has some stalk in it, and is obtained from the last *dhool*. The top qualities are poor. The percentage lies around 5%. Dhool is a technical term for leaf. After rolling and sifting the finest leaf (*first dhool*) goes to the fermentation section. The remaining leaves are rolled for another 30 minutes. After that the second *dhool* is suitable for fermentation. The third *dhool*, then, still needs to be cut — Broken tea (BT). The leaf has many veins and a flat, open blade. It is thin in consistency, and is found mainly in orthodox production. Broken Pekoe Souchong (BPS) is usually a description of a spherical rolled leaf in North Indian tea.

3. Fanning-types

With the increasing use of tea-bags, Fannings-types have gained considerable significance.

Orange Fannings (OF) and Broken Orange Pekoe Fannings (BOPF) make up the smallest siftings from the uncut leaves, in tea processing by the orthodox method, not to mention Dust. OF and BOPF stain very quickly and darkly, because

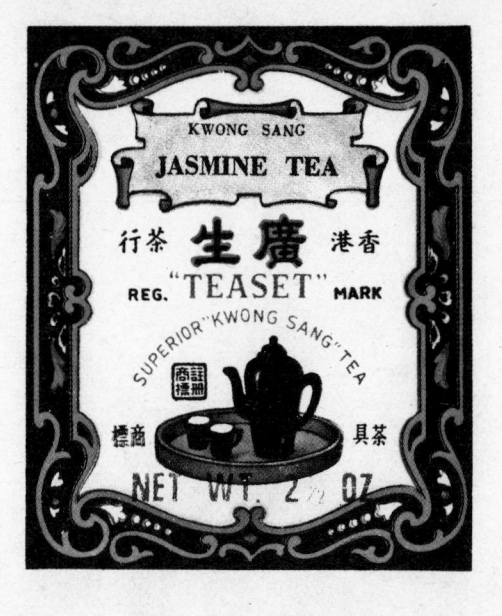

the water has free access from all sides. They often have an exceptional fragrance, especially highland tea. The quantity of BOPF is dependent on the production of BOP. Together BOP and BOPF make up 70% of the production. If 60% BOP is produced then the balance of 10% is BOPF. However, the characteristics of these two grades are different. As already mentioned BOPF gives a very strong infusion and as a rule, its leaf is pitch-black.

Pekoe Fannings (PF) — a kind of tea which corresponds with OF and BOPF and is made according to the CTC method. Very strong and fragrant, fast colouring tip quality; just like OF and BOPF it is very often used for tea-bags nowadays.

Broken Pekoe Fannings (BPF) has the same dimensions as BOPF but it is definitely inferior in

leaf appearance and is obtained from the last *dhool*. It is only brought into production if the leaves are cut, are brown in colour and very open (flat), also called flaky. Fannings (F) is a fine sifting from the various broken bits. Dust (D) and Pekoe Dust (PD) are the finest siftings. Through ignorance they are often mistaken for dust or waste. Dust makes a very strong and usually dark brew. A good D should be granular, very black and free from fibre and fannings. The *outburn* is around 3%.

Broken Mixed (BM) is a mix of flaky and regular tea. It has no fixed size, is irregular and contains a lot of stalk. The extract has absolutely no quality but does have a good colour and strength. When BM is pulverized to D, pouring qualities become a lot better. The percentage BM is dependent on the standards applied during picking. Coarse leaves can be the cause of *outburn* of around 20% BM. With precise picking this total is reduced to a minimum. With wilting there is often talk of BM production.

Green tea is mainly produced in China, Taiwan and Japan, and a Chinese will lavish much more care on his green tea than on his black. In Europe, green tea was ousted completely by black tea during the 18th century and a similar development occurred later in the United States. However, Arab countries still consume large quantities of green tea. Green tea has completely different characteristics because the fermentation process, with all its chemical changes, has not taken place. The ferment and enzymes which still remain in the tea after wilting are destroyed by high temperature steaming before the curling process and the leaves remain olive green. Japan produces panfired tea which has been placed in a bamboo basket and held briefly (1½ minutes at the most) over a kettle of boiling water. In China the following terms describe different kinds of green tea. *Gunpowder*—a very young bullet-shaped tea which has been curled. *Imperial*—curled tea from older leaves. *Hyson* means something like 'young spring' and *Young Hyson* consists of thin long leaves. *Chun Mee* indicates long leaves, *Sow Mee* the opposite—small leaves. In the tea bowl green tea takes on a lemon colour.

Oolong teas, derived from the Chinese Wu-Lung (black dragon), are semi-fermented and combine certain characteristics of both green and black tea. The best ones have a slightly peach-like flavour and because of this they are sometimes served with a peach leaf. The main supplier is Taiwan, and the main market is the United States. China produces the *Lapsang Souchong* which has a quite smoky or tarry taste. According to experts, the Lapsang of today is not what it used to be before the War when only the wood from the white fir tree was used for smoking. (Those who find the taste too overpowering can always use it in a mixture.) *Earl Grey* tea has nothing to do with the colour grey, but is actually named after the 19th century British statesman Earl Grey, who, during a diplomatic mission to China, acquired the valuable recipe for a very special Chinese mixture which, together with other ingredients, contained bergamot essence. He gave this recipe to Jackson's of Piccadilly who are still very proud of it.

In China, *Jasmine* tea, a drink that by rights should accompany every Chinese meal, is usually made from Hyson tea. (The so called 'white tea' from China will be discussed in the next chapter when we deal with the tea from the People's Republic.)

So-called fancy teas, which, despite the disdain shown to them by old-fashioned tea experts, are often sold, and make a pleasant change from the everyday teabag. We are talking now about ordinary black or green tea with an added flavour. Some of these do not keep very well. China produces different varieties of flower and fruit teas such as lemon tea (probably the most popular one in this category), lemon spiced tea (with added cloves) orange blossom tea, orange spiced tea (with orange peel and cloves) rum tea, rose-petal tea, lychee tea, grapefruit tea, raisin tea, mint tea, apple tea, mandarin tea, lotus tea, cinnamon tea, aniseed tea and nutmeg tea. Chinese scented tea has often had strongly perfumed oils added to it.

Tea is usually sold by auction, and those at Mincing Lane in London were by far the most famous, but nowadays these auctions are held at the Sir John Lyon House, High Timber Street, London E.C.4. Often the tea is auctioned in the country of origin: in Calcutta for Northern India, Cochin for Southern India, Colombo for Ceylon and Mombasa for East Africa. In the past the Netherlands used to play an important role in this field especially, of course, for tea from Java and Sumatra. The tea was auctioned in Holland in the Brakke Grond, now the Belgian Cultural Centre in Amsterdam. Before the auction the tea was stored in warehouses owned by the famous Pakhuis-meesteren van de Thee ('Warehouse masters of the tea'), a continuation of the United East India Company until the 1960's. The Netherlands still play a considerable role in the tea trade and of all the tea entering the country more is exported than consumed. The tea merchants who market the tea buy their tea through agents in the producing countries. They place their orders on the basis of samples they have tasted or standards, which are pre-defined types of tea to which buyer and seller have made certain quality agreements. Since there are over 1500 different varieties of tea in the world, skilled tea tasters are of the greatest importance. It is sometimes said that the real talent for tea tasting is present from birth; certainly the gestatory and olfactory organs have to be extremely well-developed in the tea taster and, apart from that, years of experience are required. There are well-known stories about firms fighting between themselves over one particular tea taster. Tasting is carried out on the plantation, at the auction, at the brokers and again at the tea merchants. To the outsider it appears to be an extremely complicated ritual—and so it is. The

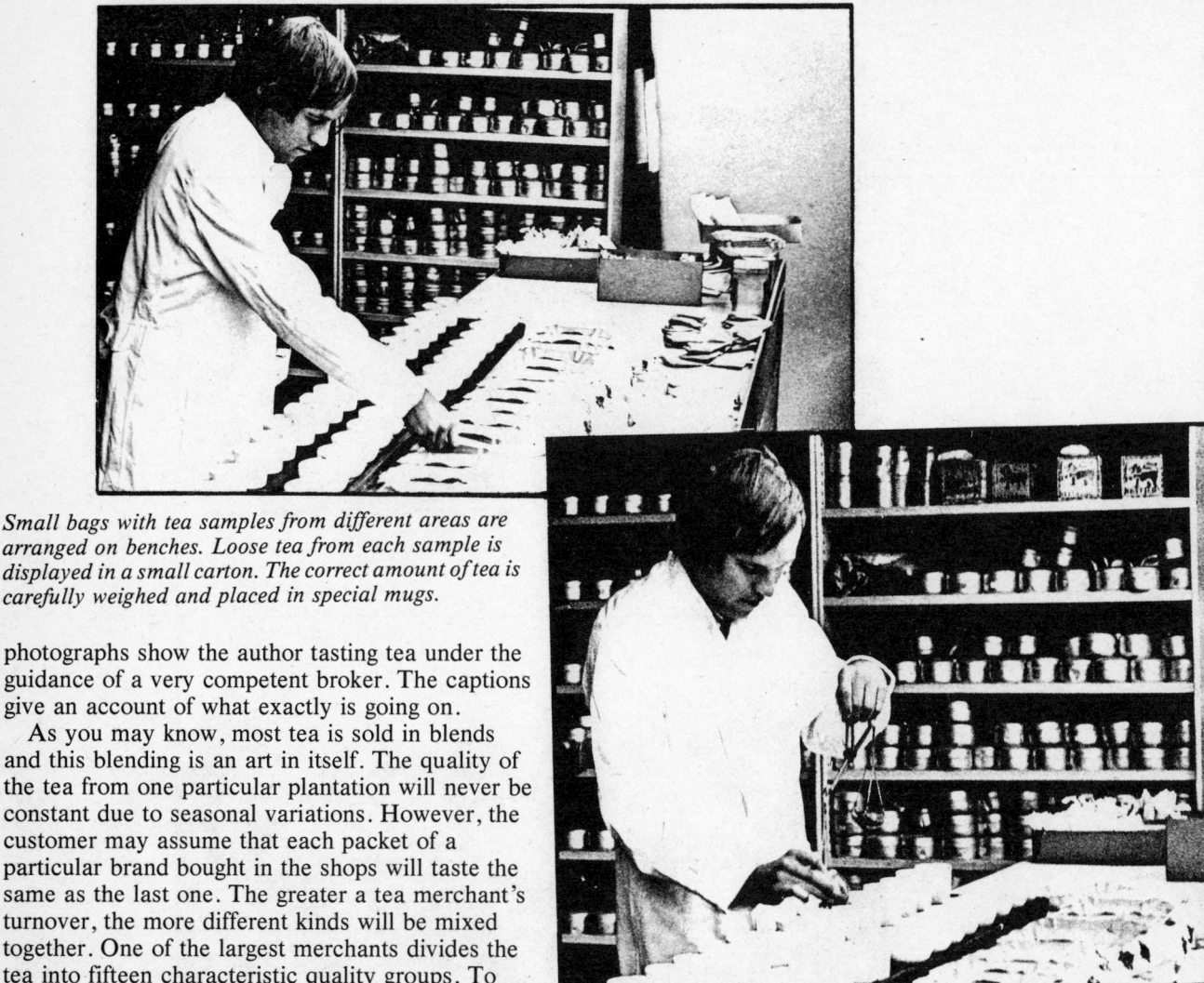

Small bags with tea samples from different areas are arranged on benches. Loose tea from each sample is displayed in a small carton. The correct amount of tea is carefully weighed and placed in special mugs.

photographs show the author tasting tea under the guidance of a very competent broker. The captions give an account of what exactly is going on.

As you may know, most tea is sold in blends and this blending is an art in itself. The quality of the tea from one particular plantation will never be constant due to seasonal variations. However, the customer may assume that each packet of a particular brand bought in the shops will taste the same as the last one. The greater a tea merchant's turnover, the more different kinds will be mixed together. One of the largest merchants divides the tea into fifteen characteristic quality groups. To prevent any one group having too much influence on the end product, eight components of 24 kinds

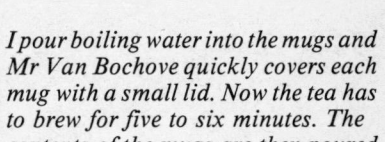

I pour boiling water into the mugs and Mr Van Bochove quickly covers each mug with a small lid. Now the tea has to brew for five to six minutes. The contents of the mugs are then poured into small bowls.

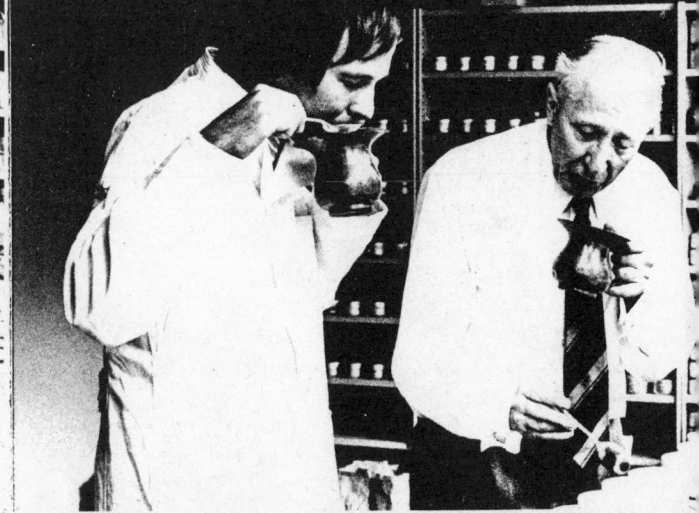

Before the tea is tasted we first smell the covered mugs to assess the flavour of the tea. The tea leaves in the mugs are turned out onto the lids, and now the tasting really starts! The bowls stay where they are; they are never

brought to the lips. Instead, a silver or silver-plated spoon is used to taste a small amount of the tea extract. And no swallowing! The tasted tea is then spewed back into a brass spittoon.

For the final assessment of the tea, the appearance (the so-called 'dry leaf'), the colour of the extracted leaf, and the colour of the extract in the bowl are all taken into consideration, as is, of course, the taste. In this way thirty or more samples are scrutinised and judged. All the equipment used is made in England.

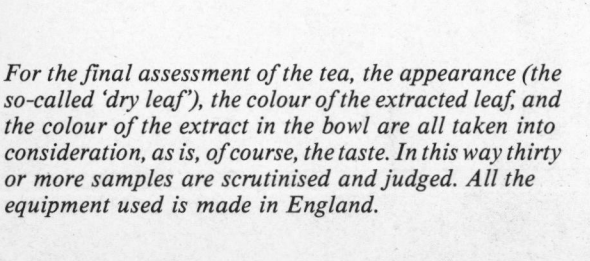

of tea each are mixed together giving a total of 192 kinds of which no single one is included at more than 1%. In this way large batches of the same composition can be made, and the replacement of one batch by another will be barely noticeable in the final product. The mixture is then stored for a while in silos. The English expression for this process is to 'marry' the tea!

Home blending can be a very rewarding occupation but don't expect to find perfect combinations immediately. A few leaves of Jasmine or Lapsang Souchong can change a dull tea into a remarkable one. A good (second flush) Darjeeling is really too good to use in a mixture. For those who want to taste a Darjeeling and have a refreshing cup of tea at the same time the best combination can be achieved by using 80% Darjeeling and 20% Ceylon blend. A refreshing and rigorous breakfast tea is blended from about 60% Ceylon tea and 35% Assam tea. For a tasty afternoon tea about 75% Ceylon tea, 20% Assam tea and about 5% Lapsang Souchong can be used.

A Glossary of Tea Tasters' Terms

Appearance

Black
Leaf black in colour, a descriptive term usually applied to low-grown teas and those made from high jat leaf. Most teas are black, but unsatisfactory withering, under-rolling and excessive handling reduces the degree of blackness.

Bold
Refers to size of leaf and indicates that the pieces of leaf are big.

Brownish
Mainly describes teas made from low jat leaf which are never really black. The term, however, may be used in the case of teas which have become brownish as a result of faulty methods of manufacture and bad plucking. See 'choppy', 'flaky', 'grey' and 'stalk'.

Choppy
Leaf chopped in a breaker or cutter rather than broken in the roller.

Even
Leaf true to grade and consisting of pieces of roughly equal size.

Flaky
Leaf not twisted, but in flakes. Results from poor withers, under-rolling and excessive breaking or cutting of the made tea, and also from the manufacture of hard leaf. Insufficient winnowing is also a contributory cause. Flaky teas do not appear as black as well-twisted leaf.

Grainy
Term applied to well-made fannings and dusts, as opposed to 'leafy'. A grade which is grainy is generally smaller in size than one which is leafy.

Grey
Leaf grey in colour. Results from too much cutting and excessive handling during sifting. Since the colour change is due to dried coating of juices on the leaf being rubbed off, a loss of some soluble matter must be expected when a tea becomes grey.

Irregular
Uneven grades.

Leafy
Used to indicate rather bold leaf in broken grades, particularly in fannings.

Make	A well-made tea, true to type and appearance.
Mixed	Leaf of different grades and size bulked together.
Open	See 'flaky'.
Ragged	A tea that is not carefully graded, being uneven and irregular in appearance and size.
Stalk	Applies to the presence of red pieces of stalk in tea. Its method of elimination obviously lies in an improvement in the standard of plucking and extra care taken in picking it out during sorting.
Tip	Term used to describe the silver or golden pieces of leaf. Unless hairs are present on the buds of a shoot tip cannot be made. Tip is a feature of low-grown teas and seldom or never enhances the value of a high-grown tea.
Wiry	Term used for a very well-twisted orange Pekoe thin leaf as opposed to 'open'.

Infusion (the infused leaf)

Bright	A good colour—not necessarily coppery. A favourable characteristic, generally denoting a good tea.
Coppery	Describes the infusion of a tea which is copper-coloured. It is more an inherent character than one developed in the process of manufacture.
Dark or dull	Dark brownish or dull green colour, as opposed to 'bright'. A derogatory term rarely associated with a good liquor, which may at times be a natural property of the leaf. Manufacturing conditions which bring it about are heat, over-fermentation and bacterial infection.
Greenish	Mainly an inherent character unless it has been the result of under-rolling and under-fermentation. A bright greenish infusion is not unfavourable.
Mixed or Uneven	An infusion of different colours. Results from mixed jat, coarse plucking and under-rolling. Hard rolling and the use of small roll-breaker mesh would bring about an improvement.

Liquor

Bakey	An over-fired tea
Body	A strong liquor as opposed to one which is 'thin'. The difference between these terms may be illustrated by the difference between watery milk and full rich creamy milk. Generally speaking,

liquors from high jat leaf. In manufacture, insufficient expression of juice from the leaf is the main cause of tea lacking 'body' or 'fullness'.

Brassy   A term seldom used for teas made by orthodox methods. May refer to a liquor with a bitter taste. A possible cause is unwithered leaf.

Bright   Bright in colour and clear, as opposed to 'dull', with some briskness.

Brisk   Having a 'live' characteristic. A tea properly fermented, correctly fired and well-preserved. Opposite of 'soft'.

Character   Prominence of some special characteristic which may be pungency, quality or flavour peculiar to the district from which the tea comes.

Coarse   A liquor which may have some strengths but is deficient in quality. Some low-grown teas are supposed to have a 'coarse' character.

Coloury   This term is used to describe a tea which possesses sufficient colour to bring it into a special category. As a rule, teas from low jat leaf are less coloury than those from high jat leaf. Colour can be improved by extension of the withering period, hard rolling and long periods of fermentation.

Cream   A cloudiness obtained when a strong tea cools.

Dry   Slight bakiness.

Dull   An undesirable characteristic in a tea mainly caused by over-fermentation. Opposite of 'bright'.

Flat   Denotes a tea that has gone off. No 'live' character and opposed to 'brisk-ness'. It is generally the result of over-exposure, and is also due to storage at too high a moisture content, or for too long a time.

Flavour   The distinctive aroma of high-grown teas, made during cold and dry weather.

Fruity   This term may denote a taint or some peculiar characteristic of tea arising from very long withers and leaf kept too long in a wet condition. The liquor acquires an over-ripe taste.

Full   A strong, coloury tea with no bitterness or coarse character.

Gone off   See 'flat'.

Greenish   A bitter taste and an unpleasant astringency. Can be caused by over-withered leaf and under-fermentation.

Harsh   Teas with too green a character.

Light   Not to be confused with 'thin'. Pale colour does not necessarily denote a poor tea. Some of the best high-grown teas are light, mainly due to a property of the leaf. A frequent cause of light liquors is tough banji. Probable manufacturing faults: over-withering, under-rolling and too short a fermentation.

Malty   An inherent character of leaf. The way in which, or the stage at which, it is developed during manufacture is still obscure. It is a desirable characteristic.

Mature   A term used to distinguish a fresh tea from one that has been stored for some time. As a result of 'post fermentation' occuring after a tea is fired, it loses some of its astringent character and becomes 'mature'. It should not be 'flat', but have a 'round' 'mellow' character.

Mellow   Opposite to 'greenish', 'harsh', 'raw', 'rasping' etc.

Metallic   See 'brassy'.

Nose   Means some aroma on the dry leaf or in the liquor. May be good or bad.

Plain   Lacking in desirable characteristics, particularly quality. Generally describes a liquor with no notable character. May be brought about by seasonal changes, rapid growths, coarse plucking or any method of manufacture which destroys quality.

Point   Accentuated briskness and a very desirable characteristic. See 'brisk'.

Pungent   Astringency without bitterness. May mean a tea with more marked 'point'. A seasonal characteristic, which can be destroyed by prolonged withering and fermentation.

Quality   Is commonly used to denote the presence of some desirable characteristics in the liquor including its appearance. For the preservation and improvement of this characteristic in a high-grown tea, the essential requirements are short withers, hard rolling and short periods of fermentation.

Rasping   Akin to 'harsh'.

Row   Same as 'harsh' and 'rasping'.

Round   See 'full' and 'mellow'.

Smooth   Means more or less the same thing as 'round'. Not so pronounced as a 'full' liquor in colour and strengths.

Soft   Teas without point or briskness. Not as poor a term as 'flat', nevertheless denotes a lack of 'life'. Mainly caused by over-fermenting, and too high a moisture content.

Sour   A sourish taste through bacterial in-
        fection. Rarely an inherent character.
        The main factors bringing about this
        characteristic are slow removal of
        surface moisture from wet leaf and
        unclean rolling and fermenting conditions.

Stewed A tea lacking in aroma with an
        undesirable liquor character, due to an
        excessive loss of essential oils resulting
        from teas being 'stewed' in the initial
        stages of firing. The remedy lies in
        thinner spreading and quicker firing at a
        higher exhaust temperature in order to
        increase the rate of evaporation of
        water.

Strong   See 'body'. Teas with good strength
(strength) cream down well and need not necess-
            arily be coloury.

Sweaty A tea with a strange and most
        unpleasant taste. A taint probably
        acquired in a similar manner to that
        described as 'fruity' and 'sour'.

Sweet   A light liquor and not of very good
        quality.

Tainted An objectionable flavour. There are
        several ways in which a taint may be
        acquired. Some may probably be ab-
        sorbed by the plant from the soil, whilst
        others may result from the spraying or
        dusting of certain insecticides. As
        distinct from these chemical taints,
        those that are produced during the
        processing of tea mostly arise from
        bacterial infection. Withering or ferm-
        enting being carried out too far under

damp, unclean conditions is generally
responsible for musty off-flavours, such
as 'sour', 'fruity' and 'sweaty'. Additional
taints may be acquired when tea comes
in contact with—or is stored in the
proximity of—odour-bearing materials
at any stage in manufacture. Some
odour taints may get volatilized in the
process of firing but a 'tatty' taint, for
example, which results from unwashed
hessian, may persist.

Tatty   A taint from hessian.

Thick   Denotes a strong liquor.

Thin   The reverse of 'thick'. A tea with little
        strength. If not the result of an inherent
        property of the leaf, lack of strength in a
        liquor is usually due to very hard
        withers, under-rolling or high rolling
        temperatures.

Washy   A very thin liquor, lacking in strength.

Weak   Similar to 'washy'.

Weathery A term descriptive of a soft character
         associated with teas made during very
         wet weather. Attributed to unsatisfactory
         withering conditions.

A modern tea factory.

Production and Consumption of Tea

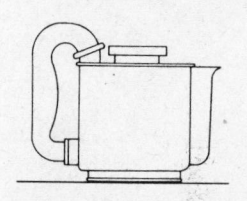

Tea is the most commonly drunk fluid after water and is the cheapest beverage in the world—this is not an advertising slogan but the truth! Here are a few figures.

Tea Production in 1980 (figures from the International Tea Committee Annual Bulletin of Statistics, all figures in 1000 tonnes.)

World Total	1,798
Asia	
India	577
China	290
Sri Lanka	191
Turkey (est)	100
Japan	102
Indonesia	79
Bangladesh	40
Taiwan	24
Iran (est)	20
Malaysia	3
Africa	
Kenya	90
Malawi	30
Tanzania	17
Mozambique (est)	19
Rwanda (est)	7
Uganda	2
Zaire (est)	6
Mauritius	4
South Africa (est)	6
Burundi	2
Cameroon (est)	2
Zimbabwe	1
South America	
Argentina (est)	34
Brazil (est)	10
Equador (est)	2
Peru (est)	3
Oceania	
Papua New Guinea (est)	8
USSR	115

Tea Imports in 1979
Figures from FAO Yearbook 1979 in 1000 tonnes. Figures relate to tea imported by each country for its own use.

EUROPE	
Britain	174
USSR	49.5
Poland	23

West Germany	14
Ireland	11
Netherlands	9
France	7
Italy	3.5
Sweden	3
Denmark	2.3

REST OF THE WORLD

Morocco	197
Libya	126
USA	78
Egypt	35.5
Iraq	26
Japan	24
Australia	23
Saudi Arabia	20.3
Sudan	20
Canada	19
Iran	19
Chile	15.5
Afghanistan	15.3
South Africa	15
Tunisia	12
New Zealand	6.6
Mongolia	6
Israel	3
World Total	1015

As we know that tea cultivation is developing rapidly in Papua New Guinea it can now be said that tea grows in five continents. (It is not grown in North America however, although experiments have been carried out in South Carolina.) In Europe, tea is only successfully grown in the Soviet Republic of Georgia along the Black Sea on the foothills of the Caucasus. Southern Europe has the right temperature but lacks the necessary rainfall of around 2500 mm i.e. 2½ metres a year. Because of this lack of rain, wine grapes flourish in these parts.

We will take a closer look first at the different countries producing tea and then at the figures on consumption.

India

India produces no less than 5,500,000 tonnes, (4,000,000 of which comes from North India, 1,500,000 from South India) of all the tea in the world and there are tea growing areas in both northern and southern India. The map of India shows *Assam* as an appendage in the north east bordering on Burma and Bangladesh. In fact it was only because of the discovery of wild tea in Assam in the last century that the British annexed the area as quickly as they possibly could. The tea from Assam has excellent keeping qualities, it suits every kind of water and is full of flavour which makes it highly sought-after in breakfast blends.

Darjeeling: a very famous tea and rightly so! If only for its supreme natural beauty a visit to Darjeeling must be a great experience, and the best tea comes from the area around Mount Kanchenjungha in the Himalayas, where, on a clear day, Mount Everest can be seen in the distance. Nearly all Darjeeling tea is grown at a height of between one and two thousand metres. At this height the lower temperature slows down the growth. The first flush grown in May and June is light and has an exquisite flavour. Even more exceptional, and

therefore often prohibitively expensive, are the second flush teas produced in June and July.

They often have a muscatel-like bouquet. The 'rain tea' picked in the period from August to October is of lesser quality because of the south-westerly monsoon. Not particularly special, but pleasantly flavoured, are the 'autumnals' produced in November and December. Production ceases from January to April due to adverse weather conditions. Very good Darjeeling tea is a rare commodity and is sometimes extremely expensive. The total amount of Darjeeling produced is difficult to assess because of the bartering trade between the Soviet Union and India. Machinery and arms are exchanged for different products including tea and much Darjeeling tea goes to Russia via these channels.

The green tea which is widely drunk in Afghanistan usually comes from the *Kangra valley* north of Delhi. The *Dooars* district lies midway between Darjeeling and Assam. This tea makes a strong cup with a good colour and is usually used for blending. The tea from southern India, which is shipped from Cochin, is refreshing and has a fairly strong fragrance. The best tea comes from the elevated plantations in the Blue Mountains of *Nilgiris* and from the mountains of *Kerala* which are situated in the south-west corner of India. which are situated in the south-westerly tip of India.

Bangladesh

Before the war of Independence in 1971 Bangla-desh produced about 2% of the total world's production. The young nation had a troubled start, with great internal disruption and the loss of the market in West Pakistan. However the situation has rapidly improved and, after jute, tea is the greatest contributor to the national revenue.

Ceylon

Ceylon, now called Sri Lanka, has a countryside and climate like paradise, but with massive political and economical problems. Apart from a small proportion of so called Burghers (an old Dutch word best translated as 'citizens' still carrying Dutch names and mainly occupied as traders) the majority of the population is Singalese. The minority of Tamils were brought to the island by the British to work on the tea plantations and it was their humble labour which made the tea industry in Ceylon what it is today. However, they are shown no gratitude. Ceylon would rather do without them and India, already over-populated, does not exactly welcome them back.

Tea is essentially a product of Third World countries (ignoring for the moment the USSR and Japan—the only two countries searching for efficient methods of mechanising the tea harvest). Taking Ceylon as an example we will now have a closer look at the problems of the Third World countries. We are dealing here with a typical mono-culture. The tea industry earns 66% of Ceylon's foreign currency and one shudders to think what the effect of a destructive disease, like the one which wiped out the coffee plantations in the last century when the island was still an English colony, would be on the tea trade. But even without a natural disaster, the situation is bad enough. For its top quality tea Ceylon will always be able to command a high price, but the position is very different for teas of average quality. In this area African competition is growing stronger. Whilst production in Ceylon is already at its full potential, the African countries still have plenty of scope to increase theirs, and in many cases they

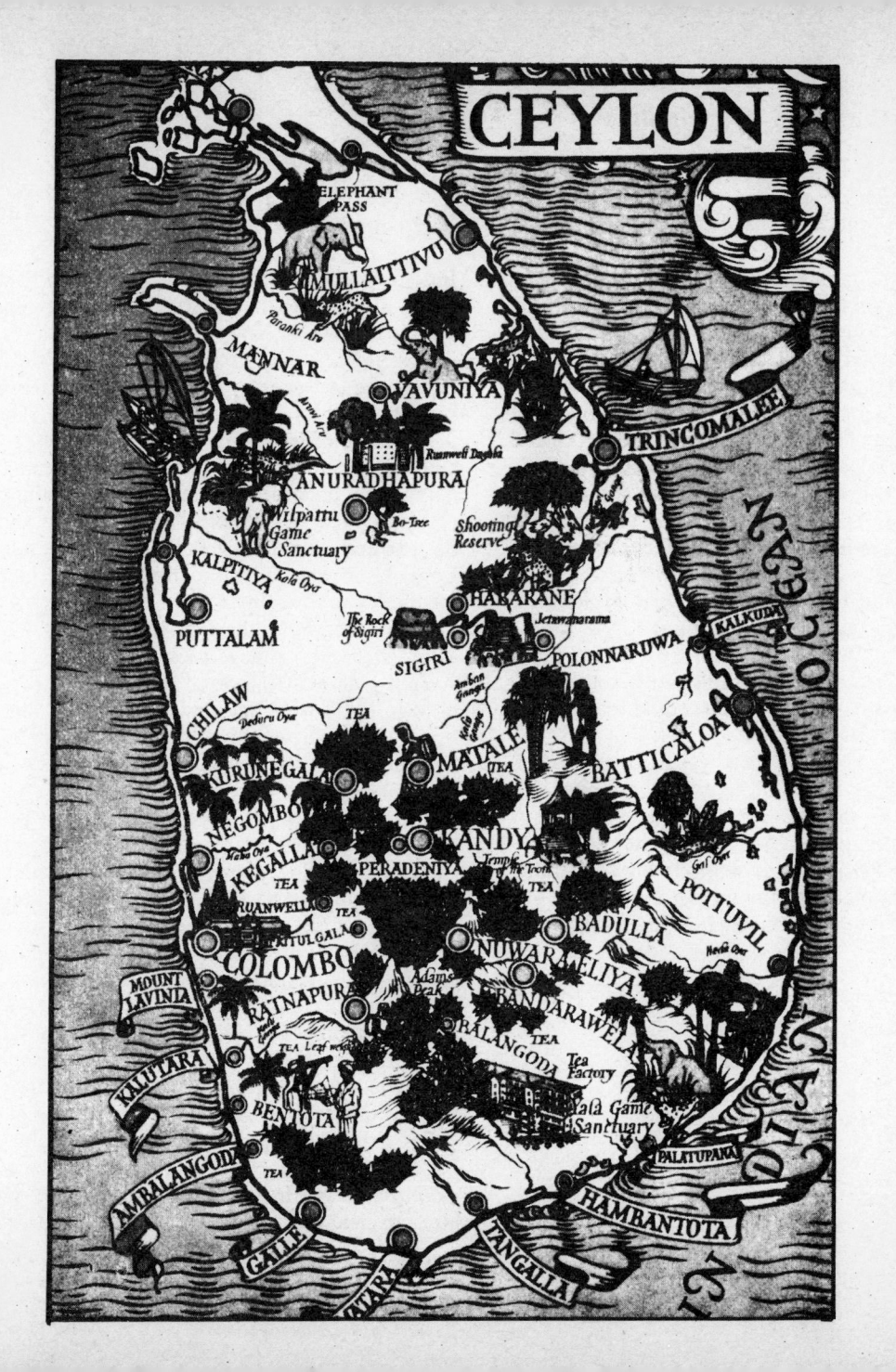

have ambitious plans in this direction for the future.

In Ceylon tea is produced throughout the year to the east of the capital Colombo and in the Galle district on the southern point. The tea is exported from Colombo and Trincomalee. From July to September the monsoon rains hit the western part of the island, but Uva and the eastern districts have dry winds. The finest Ceylon tea is produced in Uva during this period. From December to March the situation reverses. The monsoon comes from a north-easterly direction on the eastern part of the island, resulting in higher yields but lower quality tea in this area. At the same time the western part has dry winds which give rise to an excellent tea in Dimbula and Dickoya. Nuwara Eliya is a holiday resort situated right in the centre of the mountain ridge which runs north-south across the island—here an outstanding tea can be picked all year round.

Ceylon tea is generally very versatile and lends itself to blending. Four different sorts are available, distinguished by their respective areas of origin. *Nuwara Eliya* supplies the 'champagne' of the Ceylon teas. *Uva* produces a strong breakfast tea. *Dimbula* is the name of the largest tea district in Ceylon. *Kandy* tea is named after the ancient royal capital.

Indonesia

Indonesia accounts for 4% of the total world production of tea. In the Netherlands Java and Sumatra teas still have special appeal—after all it was the Dutch who first planted the tea on Java during the last century. In 1835 the frigate Algiers brought the first Java tea to Amsterdam. The plants were of the Chinese variety and the cultivation and processing were carried out completely according to the Chinese method. As a result, the tea had an excellent fragrance and flavour and a name like Bohea reappeared as Boey. However, cultivation did not prove profitable for the local government, and in 1842 it was therefore limited to the Preanger regions and Mid-Java. In 1888 a change took place when the Assam plant was imported and the British methods used in India were adopted. The quality improved rapidly and, through their considerable expertise, the Dutch secured a strong position in the international market for Java tea.

Tea is grown in the following districts: Besoeki, Cheribon, Wonosobo, Madioen, Pekalongan, Preanger and Soekaboemi. Tea from Goalpara is the most coveted and expensive. The estrangement between the Netherlands and Indonesia when the latter became independent resulted in a marked decline in tea production on Java and Sumatra both in quality and quantity. In recent years the quality has improved steadily. The processing is still orthodox: that is to say no CTC, especially since the use of the teabags in neighbouring Australia is still very limited.

In Sumatra we find tea in the districts Deli, Padang and Palembang. The island is situated on the equator and in the tea growing areas there are no rainy and dry seasons; the rain falls steadily

FREGAT ALGIERS

NEÊRL. INDIE

JAVA SOUCHON
PREANGER
REGENTSCHAPPEN
N° 2.

Tea picking in Java

throughout the year. Therefore the quality is constant with a peak in the slightly drier months (May to August and the beginning of September).

Sumatra tea is a strong tea with body, Java tea is lighter but flavoury; as the tea expert might say. *Malaysia* also produces tea although of an inferior quality. More interesting, however is the *People's Republic of China* and we should really have started with this country, the oldest tea growing nation in the world. It produces 16% of all the tea in the world with only a small proportion exported. Exports to Western Europe decreased enormously between 1880 and 1930 and those to Eastern Europe declined mainly during the sixties because of ideological differences. The home market is, of course, vast. How large is difficult to assess with any accuracy, because the figures are not published in the West, but any visitor to China will tell of tea bowls being continually refilled, usually with green tea. Traditionally, the peasants used to grow small quantities of tea on their own plot of land but these methods have altered drastically since the revolution. We will not deal here with green tea, the tea brickettes or scented tea. What we are talking about here is an unfermented tea processed in a different way from green tea. The colour in the porcelain bowl should be very clear and the tea full of flavour. The best quality is the Silvery Tipped Pekoe or Flowery Pekoe made from the so-called 'large white' tea plant and grown in the Ching Wo and Sung Chi districts of Fukien.

Black tea from China often has a reddish colour in the cup. Most westerners prefer to drink it in the late afternoon or evening rather than in the morning. The smell of the slightly sweet Keemun tea is sometimes compared to the aroma of orchids.

Yunnan in the south west (the name means 'the land south of the clouds') has only during the last twenty years developed a sizeable tea industry at altitudes of between 1100 and 2300 metres. The taste of this tea is best described as somewhere between 'real Chinese' and Assam.

As we have seen already the very first tea in the world was grown in Szetchuan. This area still produces an excellent tea—clear as springwater. From Fukien comes the strong aromatic Paklum Conou which has an orangy colour in the cup, and there are black teas from Yingteh, Kweichow, Hainan and Pingsuey. The island of *Taiwan* accounts for 0.5% of the world's production and produces mainly green tea (the most special being the semi-fermented Oolong tea from Formosa).

In *Vietnam* it was the French who originally cultivated the tea. Despite a continuous state of war for 25 years, tea is still grown and exported, although in much smaller quantities now. In the south, excellent tea is—or was—produced around Pleiku. As the guerrilla war was often fought in the plantations these have obviously suffered a great deal. In the north of the Republic tea is grown around Hanoi. It is still exported to Russia, but in the reconstruction of the devastated country tea cultivation is not one of the main priorities. Tea from *Japan* (proportion of world production 1.9%) is rarely encountered in western Europe. Small quantities of green tea are sometimes available in specialist shops but this is never the powder tea used in the ceremony. The tastiest is the Genmai-Cha Tokiwa.

In Japan boiling water is poured straight on the leaves in the bowl. Nara, Kyoto and Shizuoka are the largest production areas. The only exporting that takes place is to the United States and Morocco. Japan itself imports large quantities of green tea from Formosa.

I have come across some very interesting information about *Papua* the independent part of New Guinea. Here the tea is grown in the Waghi Valley in the western highlands where both climate and soil conditions appear to be ideal. The tea from this area is highly valued on the London market. However the majority of the tea production from Papua New Guinea is sold to Australia with only a small quantity being brought to London.

Iran and *Turkey* also grow tea in the north. I have never yet heard any praise for Turkish tea. The F.A.O.(the Food and Agricultural Organisation of the United Nations) often lays itself open to criticism by protecting such enterprises as tea cultivation in Turkey.

Within the *Soviet Union* tea is grown in Georgia, mainly for domestic consumption, although there are four different sorts of gruzinski tchai available outside the USSR. Exact figures are unknown but it would appear that the USSR consumes roughly 140,000 tonnes of tea a year of which 100,000 tonnes is estimated to be grown in the country itself. As we have seen, the rest comes mainly from India. So Russia still produces enormous quantities. In Georgia special vehicles have been introduced for mechanised pruning, a similar development to that in Japan where mechanised shears are used. However, compared with hand pruning, the results are rather crude. Apart from the fact that it is questionable whether the Georgian workers are better off working in the petro-chemical industry of Baku than on the tea plantations, it is particularly the labour-intensive nature of the tea industry that makes it so important for a Third World country like India. Mechanisation there would only result in unemployment, and a disastrous influx to the already overcrowded cities.

Africa has doubled its tea production over the last ten years and plans for the future are very ambitious. African tea now accounts for more than half of UK imports and *Kenya* is the second largest supplier of tea to the UK after India. Most, and usually the best,

Tea was first planted in Limuru at about 6000 feet in 1904 and extensive estates were developed in the highlands of Kericho and Nandi in the 1920's. Expansion in recent years had been spearheaded by the increasing production of tea by smallholders working through the Kenya Tea Development Authority (KTDA), which is now a significant producer in Kenya. The crop has increased rapidly in the last 10 years, and almost doubled to around 90,000 tonnes in 1981. Most of the production is exported, with Britain taking about half the Kenyan crop. Kenyan teas are good quality, being bright with body and excellent colour. They are widely used by blenders, and figure prominently in tea bags.

During the sixties *Uganda* was Africa's second tea-producer. The years of dictatorship under Idi Amin brought a terrible blow to the economy. Export of tea was drastically reduced. Now once more we can take an optimistic view—and the quality of high-grown tea from Uganda tends to be very good.

The small twin countries *Burundi* and *Rwanda* also went through a period of turmoil during the seventies. Recently, they have been giving priority to their tea industries. Rwandan tea, especially, can compete with the best tea in the world.

Zambia has been growing its own tea since 1974. The Kawambwa plantation is to be extended. Tea is grown exclusively for the home market.

A decade ago tea plantations were set up in *Ethiopia* with the help of western firms. These firms withdrew after the revolutionary Dergue took over. Nothing much is known about the present state of the tea-industry.

Tea picking in the eighteenth century

The *Sudan* consumes an impressive 1234 gr. per capita per year. Quite understandably it wants to grow its own tea. The FAO supports these projects, but on the whole the Sudanese climate is too dry for growing tea.

In *Malawi* the British started to grow tea during the last century when the country was still called Nyasaland. Here it is grown on the lowlands mainly in the Southern Region around the Thyolo and Mulanje Districts close to the Mozambique border. Tea was first exported from Malawi in 1905, when half a tonne was exported — today exports are around 32,000 tonnes, the principal customer being the United Kingdom. The tea, which is of medium quality, has body and thickness, and is widely used in blending. *Mozambique* also produces tea. In the Zambesi province on the Malawi border, the Portuguese planted tea in the hills. However, since 1973 production and export figures have fallen sharply.

The cause is very simple. After the liberation of the Mozambique people, the big land-owners and those Portuguese executives who had no sympathy with Frelimo left the country. The export trade from Beira Port has also decreased considerably, affecting exports from Malawi as well. The recovery of Mozambique's position on the world tea market will depend to a large extent on the developments in neighbouring *Zimbabwe*. For a long time British planters have been growing tea in the hills near the border with Mozambique. From 1965 to 1979 none of this tea could be officially exported due to U.N. sanctions. In independent Zimbabwe tea of good quality is still being grown and exports are getting a new chance. In the twenties there had been plans in *South Africa* to grow tea in Natal but this proved unsuccessful. Since 1964, however, tea has been planted round Tzaneen in north Transvaal, and in

Zululand Natal. The 'homeland' Transkei also produces tea. The quality is good and during 1976, 3,300,000 kilos were produced. The aim will probably be to supply the home market completely as the government in Pretoria has to be prepared for an eventual boycott by Third World countries.

The island of *Mauritius* is well known for the tea trade agreements signed there. The quality of its own tea is quite reasonable. The plantations have beautiful names such as Corson, Chartreuse and Marie Anguilles, more commonly associated with vineyards. Another African tea producer is *Cameroun* on the west coast.

Zaire, formerly known as the Congo, grows tea in the eastern mountains, especially the Kivu district. According to experts, some of the plantations produce very good tea but a look on the map will show that there are no sea ports anywhere near the area.

Latin people are not great tea drinkers, and the population of South America is no exception to this rule. Still it produces 2% of total world production. A small proportion comes from *Peru* and *Brazil* but *Argentina* produces most of it along its borders with Paraguay. It is lowland tea only suitable for use as bulk in the cheaper blends.

In 1980, the total production of tea in the world amounted to 1,798,000 tonnes and four times this weight was picked as fresh leaf. The total reflects a steady annual increase in world production and, unless unforeseen disasters occur, production will continue to increase to keep pace with the increase in consumption. The FAO tries to stimulate this consumption through widespread promotion. The chances of an increase are most likely in the Third World countries rather than in the industrial countries. Central and southern European countries have great potential although they are still dedicated to coffee and wine. South Americans still prefer coffee and yerba maté. There is also the possibility of a substantial increase in demand in the Middle East and in large parts of Africa.

In India, tea is becoming more and more the national drink, although traditionally tea drinking is foreign to the Hindu culture. Already India consumes half of its tea production. It is often drunk with a segment of orange in it. The tea trade agreement, arranged under FAO supervision in Mauritius in 1969, has in fact consolidated very little. Similar cocoa and coffee agreements have so far been much more effective.

I hope that the following list of figures will not be too daunting because the data on tea consumption worldwide is very interesting indeed. We will abstain from any in-depth reflection on the possible differences in character of the (contemplative?) tea drinking nations and the (emotional?) coffee drinking. All figures apply to 1978 and express the per capita consumption in grammes.

UK	3180
Denmark	430
France	120
West Germany	210
Ireland	3590
Netherlands	650
Poland	530
USSR	550
Canada	860
USA	370
Hong Kong (an indication for China?)	1760
Japan	970
Jordan	1020
Sri Lanka	1500
Algeria	770
Morocco	980
Australia	1660
New Zealand	2380
Iran	1050
Iraq	2320
Libya (1971 figure)	5473

Using quantities of imported tea as a guide, Bulgaria and Greece trail behind the rest of Europe.

I want to say more about four countries: Australia, Libya, England and the Netherlands. In Australia they consume gigantic quantities of tea and this habit is immortalised in the famous song 'Waltzing Matilda' which refers to the kettle as a Billy and the teapot as Matilda.

Libya beats all other countries of the world as far as tea consumption is concerned. In the hot dry climate the strong sweetened green tea is drunk all day long with kouskous and with shish-kebab. During the thirties Tripoli saw the start of a new preparation of tea along the following lines: a strong extract is made of black tea by boiling the leaves as often as four times. During the boiling, sugar is added continuously. This method of preparation is disastrous, because the extract is addictive and has a harmful effect on the body. Although green tea has made a comeback the consumption of this black tea is still exceptionally high.

The British and their tea is a subject to which whole books have been dedicated. The way in which we drink the tea with sugar and milk originated in France: Madame De Sévigné is alleged to have started it in the 17th century. The question of which should be put in the cup first: sugar and milk, or the tea, is often disputed. Sugar and milk first is to be preferred although conventionally this is not correct. During the Second World War the British government was very much aware of how important tea was in sustaining the morale of the troops as well as of the

Tea pavilion along the River Vecht. Engraving by Cornelis Troost.

nation. Tea was transported by the State directly from the colonies of Ceylon and India to the mother country. Churchill once said: "Tea is more important for our soldiers than ammunition.' There is a famous story about the Ford factories in

Dagenham where, in 1961, 37,000 workers went on strike because it was threatened that the morning tea break would be shortened by five minutes, and that the amount of milk in the tea was to be reduced.

There was a trend in the early sixties for the

consumption of tea to fall, particularly among young people, due to the popularity of coffee bars. Lyons tearooms ('Tea for two' because once upon a time a pot of tea cost twopence) have disappeared in England. There are signs of a tea revival now with tea dances becoming popular.

As we have seen, the first tea to reach western Europe arrived in the Netherlands, and very quickly this country became one of the greatest tea drinkers in the world. Tea was drunk in all circles and districts but the 'institution' of afternoon tea parties was established first and foremost amongst the upper class families, especially in The Hague. The following quote describes the procedure: 'In The Hague one would set out for a tea party three hours past noon, no overcoats were worn although a loose cape might be used on rainy days. Thus one would be seated immediately on the chairs provided and foot stoves would be available in summer as well as in winter. Now the hostess would take some small intricately-painted porcelain or silver filigree tea caddies containing different sorts of tea—each would be brewed in separate small porcelain tea pots and poured through silver tea sieves in delicate little cups so as to allow the visitors to judge the tea of their choice'.

During the War tea was drunk weaker and weaker and sugar and milk were gradually omitted. Later on, only cubes of tea dust euphamistically called 'Santé' were available. Finally, one had to resort to herb teas. After the War coffee was rationed for much longer than tea—for some reason

THE CUP THAT CHEERS BUT NOT INEBRIATES.

ROBINSONS BRISTOL. 394

people were inclined to spend more money on the apparently more valued coffee. At the same time, through a false economy, the use of weak tea persisted, in many cases until the present day. Tea is still amazingly cheap considering the care which is taken with the product from the plantation to the tea factory. The introduction of the tea bag did not help, because one bag of 4 gr is too small for the customary Dutch tea pot of around 1 litre. In the evening tea has been ousted almost completely by coffee (except in Friesland where this development is only just beginning).

A fairly recent survey has shown that tea is drunk at breakfast time by 83% of adults questioned, in the late afternoon by 64%, with the evening meal by 40%, and at night by 25%. Incidentally, I personally do not think that sugar in tea is a good idea and would advise anybody to try and cut down in order to get more of the taste of the tea itself. Cane sugar would be preferable as it is not as sweet as beet sugar. The recent development of a cult of tea drinking deserves a special mention. This is a trend which started in the early seventies and was in no way propogated by advertising; a comforting thought which shows that the consumer is not completely the victim of advertising. The causes of this tea cult are not entirely clear. They are probably related to overland trips to India and to a preference for an exotic drink which by its nature is better suited to a time of Neo-Frugality and contemplation than coffee with its stronger, stimulating effect. A short-lived fashion or an established habit? I would think the latter. The patterns of taste have widened too: herb teas and fancy teas (lemon, mint, jasmine, Lapsang, etc) are more popular. With a bit of luck and some good water the first class Darjeeling and the exquisite Chinese teas may be rediscovered as well ... A good time will then be ahead of us!

The Tea Set

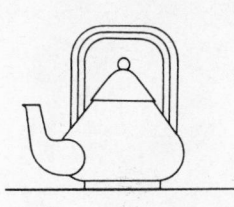

In a book on tea the history of the teapot should not be omitted. I would mention a book by John Bedford called 'All about Teapots', an excellent and well laid out little book which, through its extensive list of literature, will direct the reader further.

The Ch'a Ching recommends a high teapot like a wine pitcher, but this did not prove very efficient since its short spout soon became blocked with tea leaves. The first teapots were made in the village of Yi-Hsing on the shores of Lake Taihu, not far from Shanghai. These inconspicuous little pots were exported first to Japan and later to Europe. Porcelain was invented in China during the T'ang dynasty (620–907). However very little has survived which originated from before the Ming era (1368–1628). The industry was centred mainly around Nanking. In 1510 the first Japanese porcelain was manufactured from Chinese raw materials. Later on, Japanese stone is used. In Japan the porcelain centre is Arita, and a direct influence on the Dutch Delft pottery can be traced via the Dutch trading post on the island of Decima in the bay of Nagasaki. Japanese exports to Holland however, consisted mainly of the rather coarser pots made in Imari. In Delft the first attempts were made to imitate Chinese teapots; in 1659 by Aelbrecht de Keiser, a master potter, and later by Arij de Milde

who used a fox as his trade mark. In Delft small pots for either one or two cups were made. The Dutch brothers Elers brought the art to Staffordshire. As this Delftware was really too fragile for teapots, there is unfortunately little of it left.

In the meantime Europe was importing pottery and porcelain from China on a large scale. It wasn't valued very highly and in the holds the tea sets were usually at the bottom with the tea above it and the silk on top.

In 1780 the Dutch United East India Company had orders for 1,134,200 porcelain items which included 450,000 cups and saucers.

The 'Chine de Commande', which was made in China after European designs is world famous. It is remarkable how accurately the Chinese craftsmen depicted a world totally strange to them although the occasional mistake was made. One mistake occurred when the Swedish town of Gothenburg, having ordered plates with the coat of arms of the town (a lion), received a consignment with a picture of a naked man! And when a rich Swedish family who ordered a set of plates with their coat of arms received them adorned with the motto "Today Mother's temper is worse than usual." The order had been sketched on a page torn from the daughter's diary.

A set of 25 Chinese plates depicting different stages of tea processing.

August the Strong, Elector to the Saxons and King of Poland, wanted to produce copper and gold cheaply so he could buy the most beautiful Chinese porcelain. The alchemist Friedrich Böttger was locked up inside a fortress to realise this dream. His friend Count Von Tschirnhaus came to his aid. He discovered how to copy the porcelain and, after great effort, he finally succeeded. The European equivalents of Kaolin (China clay) and petunse (china stone) were discovered in Saxony. In Meissen, a factory was founded which produced the famous Dresden porcelain.

Madame de Pompadour instigated the manufacture of French porcelain at Sèvres, where very clever imitations of the Japanese Imari porcelain were made. Charming little oval teapots complemented by matching sugar pots and milk jugs, were also produced. These formed either a 'solitaire' (one cup and saucer) or a *tête à tête* (with two cups). A lot of the Sèvres designs were inspired by China: European interpretations of a distant, unreal Cathay with little Chinese men and women and gardens full of flowering plum trees.

Porcelain was also made in England. The most

famous name of course is Josiah Wedgewood who joined the firm Wieldon in 1754. He dramatically changed the traditional cream-coloured earthenware (flint porcelain) which was made in Leeds and Staffordshire until then. The greatest contribution the British have made to the ceramics industry is the invention of a way to print designs on porcelain and earthenware by using paper stencils made on copper plates. Using this process Thomas Turner started the mass production of willow pattern pottery, depicting the star-crossed love of Chang and Koong-se. Wedgwood pottery is world famous, especially the blue and white bisque (unglazed) reliefs of nymphs and goddesses after classical designs. Then follows the period of Neo-Classicism sparked off by the excavations of Pompei and Herculaneum. John Spode (1754–1827) is claimed to be the inventor of the so-called 'Bone China' made from China clay, cornish stone and bone ash. It is strong and can be painted in vivid colours.

From the very beginning in Yi-Hsing, teapots were made in the strangest shapes and this habit persists: we find rattle snakes, water buffaloes, fire engines etc. A handle over the top of the pot is typically Japanese. One of the aims has been to construct foolproof lids which will not tumble into the tea cup during pouring by making a small hole in the lid. Another device was to allow some air into the pot to prevent dripping. Attempts have been made almost continuously to separate the leaves from the tea automatically after brewing. In 1901 the Earl of Dundonald acquired a patent on the S.Y.P. (simple yet perfect), a tilting teapot which separated leaf from the tea automatically by resuming an upright position after a cup had been poured (see figure 6 on page 76). Although I would not recommend their use myself, silver teapots have always been very popular in England and America.

The pear-shaped model originates from the time of Queen Anne. Other common designs were octagonally-shaped or lamp-shaped with straight spouts.

Paul Revere, immortalised by Longfellow in the poem about his midnight ride, was famous for his silver teapots. Our ordinary kettle (with lid and spout) probably goes back to a primitive type of Chinese teapot. The handle on the teacup, however, is a purely European invention. A small bowl in a lacquered holder is typically Japanese. The Russians started to drink tea from a glass, often in a silver holder in the beginning of the 18th century, quite a good idea especially for lemon tea, probably more suited to the evening than the morning. Since 1730 the tea and the coffee cup have developed along different lines in Western Europe. Personally I prefer to drink top-quality Chinese tea from a small *mokka cup* rather than a big tea cup! The

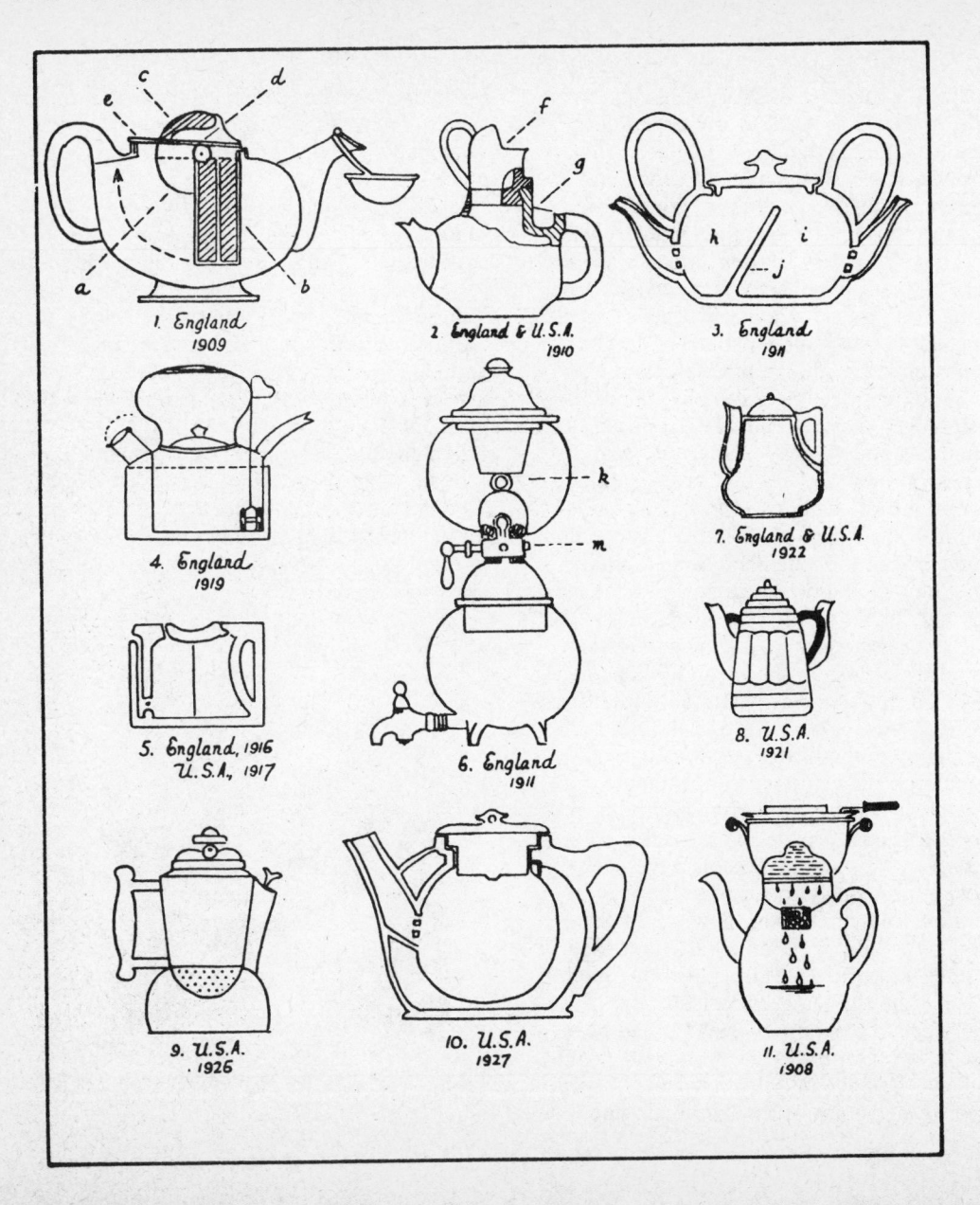

1. England
1909

2. England & U.S.A.
1910

3. England
1911

4. England
1919

5. England, 1916
U.S.A., 1917

6. England
1911

7. England & U.S.A.
1922

8. U.S.A.
1921

9. U.S.A.
1925

10. U.S.A.
1927

11. U.S.A.
1908

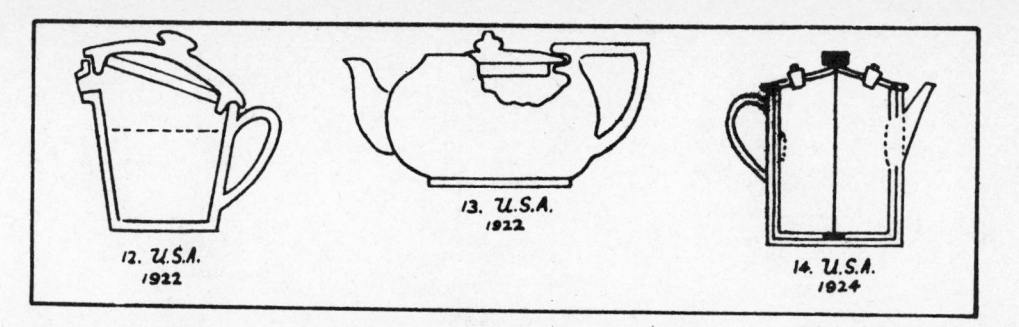

12. U.S.A.
1922
13. U.S.A.
1922
14. U.S.A.
1924

Leeds Teapot 1775

Bohea
Tea
Green
Tea

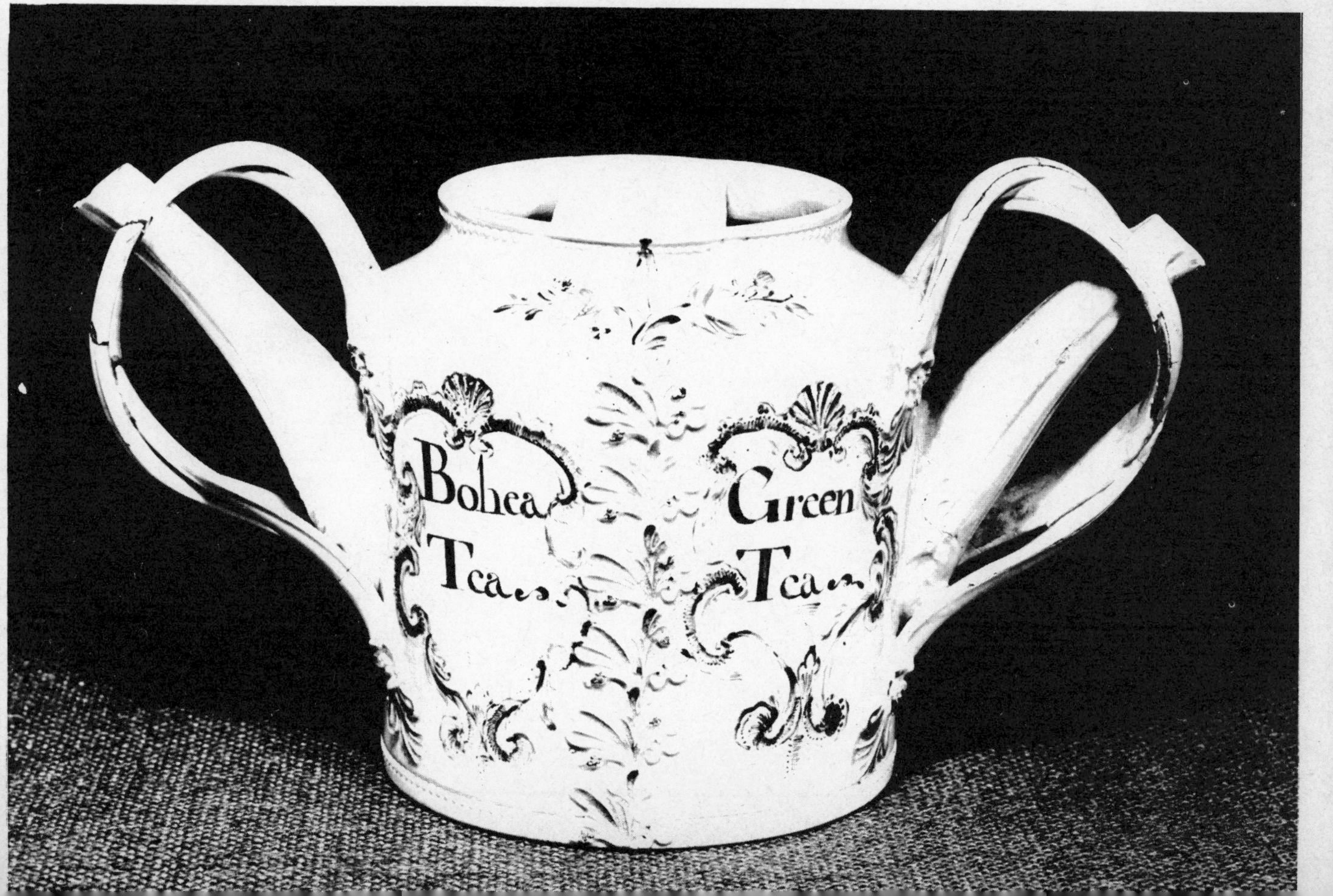

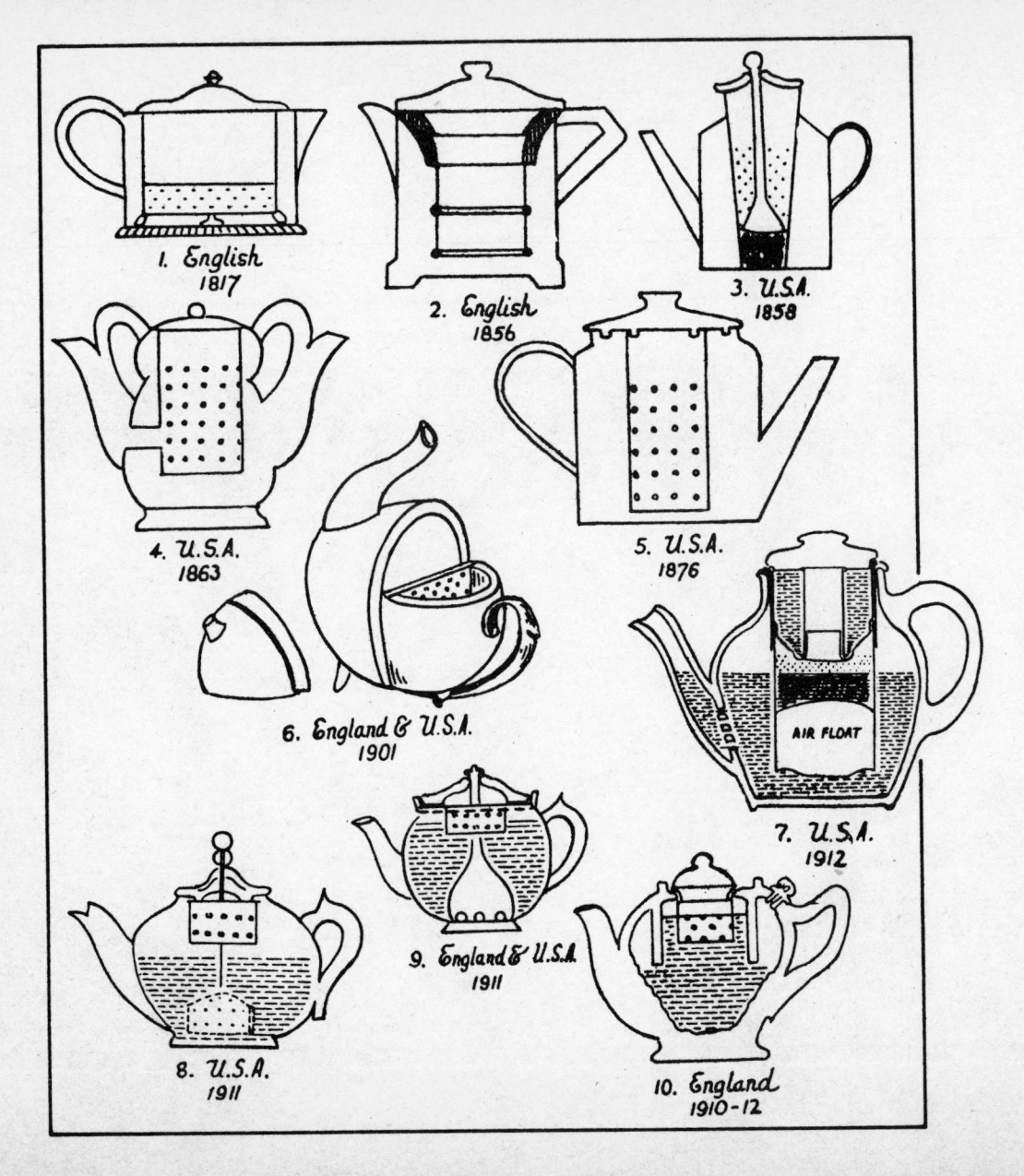

1. English 1817

2. English 1856

3. U.S.A. 1858

4. U.S.A. 1863

5. U.S.A. 1876

6. England & U.S.A. 1901

AIR FLOAT

7. U.S.A. 1912

8. U.S.A. 1911

9. England & U.S.A. 1911

10. England 1910-12

teaspoon has been a Western European addition to stir in the sugar and the milk, a fashion started by Queen Anne. 18th century tea caddies were often very ornamental masterpieces and can be seen in many museums. Unless teabags are used, or the teapot has a built-in tea sieve or container, a separate tea sieve is required as well. A silver one, of course, looks best. So-called tea eggs, perforated metal containers for loose tea, are not really a very good idea. For one thing, larger tea leaves don't have enough room to expand. It would be much better to use a tea filter akin to the coffee filter, which fully separates the leaves from the tea extract. The proper way to ship tea is in cases lined with aluminium foil because tea is easily tainted by other smells. Cloves, melons, apples and many other things should be kept well away. At home, tea is best kept in a proper tea caddy or in a simple wooden box. In general plastic and metal do not agree with tea: another objection against the tea egg. (This does not seem to apply to the same extent to the extremely elegant Japanese cast iron teapots which usually stand on a matching pot warmer fuelled by glowing charcoal.)

The word Samovar is immediately associated with Russia. It means something like 'self boiler'. The samovar, a large elegant kettle made from copper, brass or silver, is heated by a metal pipe which runs vertically through the centre of the samovar and brings the water to the boil. It has a flat plate-like top on which the teapot stands. The tea leaves in the pot are barely covered with boiling water — the tea then has to brew for five to six minutes. The extract is then poured into a jug which is kept warm on the top alongside the teapot. A small amount of the extract is poured in a glass and topped up with water from the samovar to the required strength and colour.

As we have seen, tea is best brewed in a porcelain or earthenware pot, glass teapots however are quite attractive too, and very suitable for use with teabags, which can be removed when the desired strength is seen to have been reached. A technical miracle and one of the few successful descendants of the Heath Robinson contraptions which proliferated in Britain in the beginning of the 19th century is the Teasmaid which has your morning cup of tea ready waiting for you when the alarm goes off.

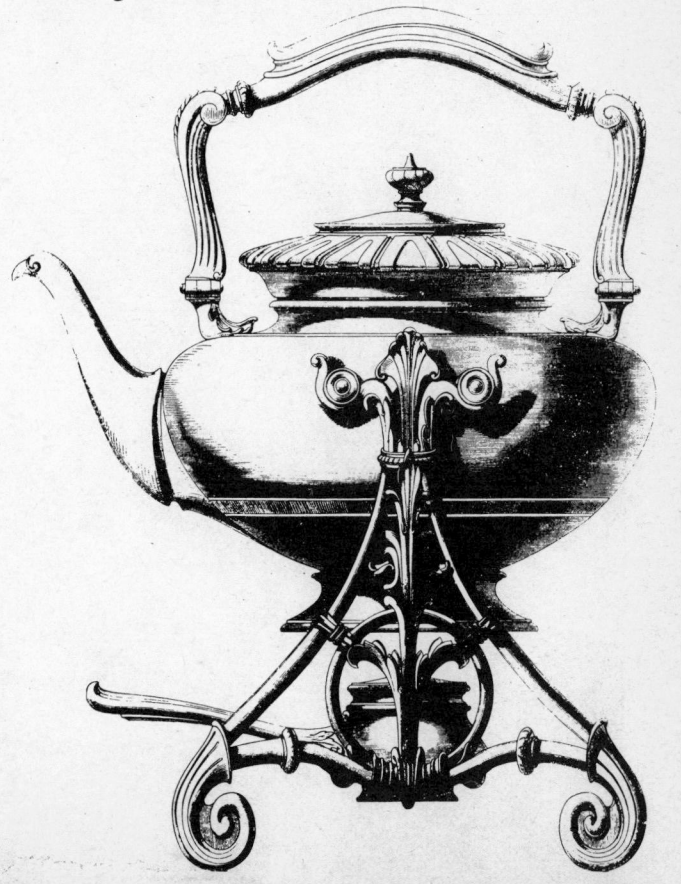

Making Tea and Tea Recipes

1. Warm the teapot by swilling it with hot water.
2. Put in one teaspoon or one teabag per cup.
3. Use fresh water: do not use more than necessary for the number of cups you are making. Pour on the water as soon as it boils.
4. Let it brew for five to seven minutes.
5. Stir the tea before pouring it out.
(Add sugar for the aroma and milk for the mild taste.)

Soap and detergents are arch enemies of tea. Keep the teapot clean with fresh water! In case the pot does get dirty for one reason or another the best remedy is to soak it overnight in a soda solution.

These quantities make a fairly strong—but by no means bitter—tea, and after all weak tea just means less flavour. 'One for the pot' can be added to taste. Most teapots hold about 1 litre and a full pot requires 8 to 10 gms of tea to a litre of fresh boiling water.

Pour on the water as soon as it boils, we have said, but this does not always apply. For a well-flavoured, tasty cup of tea we really need soft water (but not artificially softened) — water with a low calcium content. Rain water is very soft and therefore perfect for brewing tea. On a state visit to France the Queen had a special supply of Scottish rainwater brought over with her. The calcium content of the water is determined mainly by the geology of the catchment area, although it is possible to reduce the level artifically before it reaches the consumer. Hard water makes the tea cloudy and will form a thin skin on the surface. It also impairs the aroma and the taste. The hardness can be greatly reduced by boiling the water for three to five minutes—this is the time needed for brewing. Five minutes is generally ideal. Darjeeling tea needs a little longer: seven to eight minutes as do all the Flowery Orange Pekoes. The easiest way to be accurate is to set an egg timer.

Anyone suffering from constipation should avoid too much tannin. This can be done by letting the tea brew for no longer than three minutes because the caffeine is extracted before the tannin. Green, and thus unfermented, tea should never be left to brew for more than three minutes! In the Netherlands the tea is often left to brew on a so-called 'tea-light', a pot warmer fuelled by a night light candle. Let me put it this way: on no account should the tea ever be allowed to boil as this liberates far too much tannin!

A very good method is to brew tea on steam: the Japanese method of using smouldering charcoal is fine too. The tea cosy should be a snug fit to allow optimum conditions for brewing.

Making tea for large numbers of people is not so easy, generally the smaller the quantity made at any one time the tastier it will be. (In the back of the book there is more information on this topic in the list of addresses and literature.)

The addition of sugar and milk is typically English. Since the War this habit has died out in the Netherlands. It is by no means essential even for a strong cup of tea although milk does precipitate the tannin! The same rules apply more or less to the use of teabags. Most bags contain 3.13 gm of tea and therefore at least two should be used in a 1 litre teapot. Unless otherwise stated the teabags should be left to brew for about six minutes, then stirred around and removed. Tea bags were accidentally discovered by Thomas Sullivan, a tea importer in New York. As an economy measure, he began in 1908 to send his clients tea samples in small silk bags rather than in the usual tins which were a lot larger. To his amazement he was inundated with orders, not so much for his tea, as for the practical little bags. This was the beginning of the teabag.

There are two types of bags: first of all, the floating bag which is very simple and most common in Britain. In earlier days the main objection against this bag was the lingering taste of glue. Of course this would be noticed at once by the professional tea taster who considered it beneath his dignity to market this type of bag. These days we have the heat sealed process which has eliminated the taste of glue. There are now also 'string and tag' teabags which have always been more common in Europe. The tea is easily extracted from this type of bag.

The German who walked out of East Germany and went to Dusseldorf with the idea for the construction of the machine producing these

A CLOCK THAT MAKES TEA!

And tells you when it is ready.

(Patent.)

Prices 25/- to 70/-.

Please send for Illustrated Booklet of this most Ingenious and Useful Appliance, post free from—**AUTOMATIC TEA MAKER CO., 26 B, Corporation Street, Birmingham.** London Office and Showroom: 31, George St., Hanover Square, W.

bags, has become a millionaire through its patent. The machine is very ingenious. At first sight it is horrifyingly expensive, but there is an enormous demand for it. The average machine produces 14,000 packets of 20 bags at 3.13 gm per day. A machine packing loose tea can usually manage 30,000 packets of ¼ lb. The staples which hold the double bag together are totally harmless. Of course tea in bags is more expensive than loose tea. However the convenience which these days is so important, has to be paid for. Furthermore loose tea was often blamed for blockages in the waste pipe from the sink. (By the way, I hope people

with a garden realise that tea leaves make an excellent fertiliser for roses and hydrangeas.)

And what about the quality of tea sold in bags?

The Sunday *Observer* published a survey on the situation in Britain on 13th June 1971, which found the quality lacking even with the better known brand names. The quality in the Netherlands appears to be higher and indeed, British tea experts sometimes claim that the average packet of tea in the Dutch supermarket is better than that on offer to the English housewife.

The choice is also much smaller than for loose tea and all teabags contain 'dust' or 'fannings'. Tea is not a commodity that can be kept indefinitely; packets can be kept for a year, bags lose their flavour after four months.

It has to be admitted that the smaller the leaf the stronger the brew, but the strength of the tea is not the only criterion for the enjoyment derived from a 'cuppa'. With instant tea one can hardly talk about enjoyment. In the United States where a lot of iced tea is drunk there is a big market for it, but as far as I am concerned it can stay over there! One of the slightly better ones is Cey-Tea which is fabricated from unfermented green leaf on the plantations in Ceylon.

Iced Tea

An Englishman trying to sell tea from the British colonies to the public at the world exhibition in St. Louis in 1904 was driven to despair by a persistent heatwave which caused all passers-by to ignore him completely in their search for ice-cold refreshment. He put ice cubes in the tea and iced tea was born. In hot climates, especially in the southern states of America, it has really taken off. For best results the tea should be brewed to twice its usual strength and whilst still hot should be poured into tumblers filled to the brim with ice cubes. A delicious variation can be obtained by adding some mint to the tea.

An old fashioned tea lover shuddered at some of the following tea recipes even without having tasted them and I must admit that I wouldn't risk a good Darjeeling on any of them, but experimenting with tea is up to the individual and with some fantasy and dexterity, quite acceptable brews can be concocted! 'The 'Tea Cookbook' by William I. Kaufman (see literature) has the largest number of serious and quite ridiculous recipes as well as all sorts of recipes for biscuits, cakes and savouries to accompany tea.

Tea Recipes

Russian Tea—a recipe from Simon Levelt:

Heat up honey, cloves and cinnamon stick in some water in the teapot. After seven minutes add about 12 gm of tea and one litre of water which has boiled for five minutes. Leave to brew for five minutes then add some lemon and orange juice while stirring. Pour out this strong spicy drink into glasses through a tea sieve.

Persian *Lovedrink* a recipe from Simon Levelt:

Boil fresh water from three to five minutes. Pour one litre onto about 12 gm of Ceylon tea. Leave it to brew for five minutes then stir in 18 gm of sugar until dissolved and let the brew cool to room temperature. When it cools down it should be served in tall glasses containing some peach segments, a slice of orange and a measure of rum topped up with ice cubes.

Herb Tea: a recipe from Niemeijer:

100 gm of tea
3 tablespoons grated lemon rind
1 teaspoon cloves
to be mixed together and left in an airtight tin for five days.

Arabic Tea a recipe from the Dutch magazine *Avenue*:

Use a small silver teapot for preference. Put 10 sugar cubes in the bottom (for Arabic tastes this is still on the low side) add six measures of green tea and six peppermint leaves (or a pinch of dried mint). Pour over enough boiling water for six small Arabic tea glasses (available from oriental shops). Leave this to brew and once poured out it can be dusted with freshly milled pepper. However the last addition is optional!

Orange Tea: a recipe from Douwe Egberts:

Ingredients: 16 gm tea
100 gm preserving sugar
the juice from one lemon and two oranges
one teaspoon each of grated lemon and orange rind

Preparation: boil fresh water for 3 minutes, use 16 gm tea or 4 teabags to 1 litre boiling water. Let the tea brew for five minutes: cool to room temperature, add the juice and grated rind and let the mixture settle in the refrigerator. Before serving, pour the ice-cold orange tea into a jug or carafe leaving the sediment behind. This drink should be served in high glasses with clinking ice cubes ... a true pleasure!

Flambe Tea: a recipe from the Ceylon Tea Centre:

For four persons:
4 glasses Ceylon tea normal strength,
a few cloves
cinnamon
rum
Make a pot of Ceylon tea at normal strength and pour it into the lgasses. Put the crushed cloves and the cinnamon in a large ovenproof bowl. Pour the rum on top and set light to it. Pour a little of this mixture in each glass and add sugar to taste.

Mint Tea—a recipe from the Tea Cookbook.

2 springs of fresh mint
⅓ cup of fresh or unsweetened orange juice
the juice of two lemons
two cups of strong hot tea
⅓ teaspoon of ginger powder
⅓ cup of hot water
1 cup cold water
Crush the mint leaves in a bowl, pour over the fruit juices and the hot tea. Stir the ginger into the hot water and mix this with cold water. Then add the mixture to the fruit juice and tea. Let it cool for about 1 hour. Sufficient for five people.

Hot Spiced Afternoon Tea—a recipe from the Tea Board of India

4 pints water
½ level teaspoon whole cloves
half a stick of cinnamon
half pint orange juice or squash
juice from two lemons
Cinnamon sticks to serve
Put the cloves in the water and bring to the boil. Pour this over the tea and leave it to brew for five minutes. Then stir and pour it through a sieve over the sugar until the latter has dissolved. Add the fruit juices. If necessary it can be warmed on a low heat before serving. Don't let it simmer or boil. Serve with sticks of cinnamon. Sufficient for 12 people.

Tea Sorbet a recipe from the Tea Council in London:

¾ oz of good quality tea
half pint boiling water
6 oz candied sugar
juice of two lemons
half an egg white
To garnish, some sprigs of mint.
Method: leave the tea to brew for 5 minutes in freshly boiled water. Use a muslin bag to sieve the extract and melt the sugar in the hot tea. Leave it to cool and add the lemon juice. Freeze quickly in the freezer compartment of the fridge set at the lowest possible temperature or in the freezer. When the liquid is half frozen, carefully mix in the beaten egg white and leave it to freeze completely. Serve the sorbet, which should be soft, and definitely not rock hard, in pre-cooled glasses, after having dipped the rims in crème de menthe (or lemon juice) and sugar. Garnish the glasses with the mint.

Savoy Safari a recipe from the Tea Council in London, originally invented by the head barman of the Savoy Hotel in London.

1½ oz gin
½ oz strong tea (the more cautious amongst us could use 1½ oz of each)
A pinch of Angostura bitters
A pinch of pure vanilla essence powder
Mix and let it cool.
Pour the mixture into the tumbler with ice cubes and add lemonade to taste.

Veluwe Grog a recipe from Niemeijer

Put two cups of hot strong tea in a large bowl together with the juice of three lemons and six oranges and 250 gm of sugar. Stir the mixture well until the sugar is dissolved completely. Add ¼ litre of Curaçao liqueur and ¼ litre of burgundy wine.

Bring to boiling point only: on no account should the mixture be allowed actually to boil. Serve in tea glasses.

Under the heading 'Tea drinking in Tibet' I mentioned the thick soup-like tea made with yak butter and various other ingredients. I cannot imagine anybody wanting to try and make this so have therefore omitted the recipe.

TEA & ITS EFFECTS.

EXTRACTS

from a valuable & curious Book,

Preserved in the British Museum,

and presented by GEORGE IV, on

"THE QUALITIES & VIRTUES OF TEA."

IT APPEARS TO HAVE BEEN PRINTED ABOUT THE YEAR 1660.

Vide "TEA", *by G.G. Sigmond, M.D.*

"It is proper both for Winter and Summer, preserving in perfect health until extreme old age."

"It maketh the body active and lusty."

"It helpeth the Headache, giddiness, and heaviness thereof."

"It removeth the obstructions of the Spleen."

"It taketh away the difficulty of breathing; opening obstructions."

"It is good against Tipitude, Distillations, and cleareth the sight."

"It removeth lassitude, and cleanseth and purifieth acrid humours, and a hot liver."

"It is good against crudities, strengthening the weakness of the ventricle or stomach, causing good appetite and digestion, especially for persons of corpulent body, and such as are great eaters of flesh."

"It vanquisheth heavy dreams, easeth the frame, and strengtheneth the memory."

"It prevents and cures agues, surfits, and fevers."

"It strengtheneth the inward parts, and prevents consumption."

"It is good for colds, dropsys and scurvys; purging the body by sweat, and expelleth infection".

"It has been sold in England as high as Ten Pounds for one pound weight."

Chemical and Pharmacological Aspects of Tea

The constituents of Tea:
The processed tea leaves to which we will limit ourselves are made up of the following constituents:
Caffeine 2–5% (with an average of 3.5%)
Tannin or tannic acid 8–20%
Cellulose 10%
Nitrogen 4%
Fat 1.5%
Ash 5%

It is obvious from these figures that the composition of tea leaves can vary considerably. Although the constituents of the tea may be known accurately, much less is certain about the way they interact, weaken, strengthen or complement each other, and how therefore their characteristic effect on the human organism is determined.

Tea is also a subject which has been largely ignored by scientists in the last few decades. Very different from the times of Dr. Morissot, Dr. Paulli and Dr. Bontekoe, when the arguments around the new exotic beverage were fought out with fervour; to some it was a malicious poison, to others a panacea for all ailments. It was mainly due to the caffeine that tea used to be prescribed as a medicine in the past. The anti-narcotic, stimulating effect was only too clear. In 1820 Runge isolated caffeine from coffee beans and in 1827 Ondry did the same with tea leaves. Ondry assumed he had discovered an unknown substance which he called theine. However in 1837 Mulder proved that caffeine and theine were in fact identical. In a way it is quite surprising to find that tea contains more caffeine than coffee. Even so, tea has quite a different effect from coffee; tea is stimulating but not exciting! What is the reason for this difference? In coffee, by-products, produced during the roasting process, cause the caffeine to be absorbed by the body all at once. The effect of coffee is therefore very quickly noticeable and quite strong. The caffeine in coffee affects the circulation by stimulating the heart. It is because of these roasting by-products, which in very sensitive people can cause indigestion that doctors often prescribe caffeine-free coffee. The caffeine in tea does not affect the circulation via the heart but has a direct effect on hearing and the central nervous system. It makes you more alert and increases mental activity. The capacity to interpret the informational input from the senses is increased, thoughts become clearer and quicker, mental fatigue is relieved and reaction speed is significantly increased. This may seem slightly exaggerated, but tests have been carried out on groups of people doing arithmetical additions of comparable difficulty before and after drinking tea. Afterwards they needed about 25% less time to complete the series and the number of mistakes made also went down by 25%. There is no reason at all for avoiding tea in the evening out of fear of a sleepless night. Usually, there is a considerable time lapse between tea drinking and going to bed, anyway. I dare say that for every arduous task—and that includes mental activities—tea is essential. The stimulating effect of a cup of tea lasts for quite a long time and never causes any unpleasant withdrawal symptoms or 'hangovers' later on.

The second most important component of tea is tannic acid or tannin. This slows down and regulates the effect of caffeine in such a way that it is absorbed very slowly by the body with the result that the effects remain noticeable for longer and diminish very gradually. The chemical name for these substances are 'polyphenols' to distinguish them from the phenolic substances occurring in tree bark which form the true tannic acid used for tanning leather. Although the tannin in tea has certain chemical properties and precipitates gelatin and skin in powder form out of a solution, it will not change animal skins into leather and stories about the stomach lining turning to leather through excessive use of tea are nothing but old wives tales! The tannic acid content of tea has little influence on the quality; taste and aroma are the determining criteria in the end. Many of the finest Keemun and Ninchow teas from China are very low in tannin and their fame is due solely to their taste. The more accurate the picking, i.e. 'two leaves and a bud', the lower the tannic acid content. In the Dutch province of Friesland a lot of firms make a special line of coarse Orange Pekoe because it has a low tannin content—the Friesians have a habit of letting the tea simmer on all night!

In the processing of black tea quite a lot of tannin is lost during fermentation or oxidation. This does not occur with the green tea and therefore green tea should never be brewed for more than three minutes! The tannin substances make the tea slightly astringent, the astringent taste can be eliminated by the use of milk: tannin is precipitated by the protein in the milk. Apart from the main constituents (caffeine and the polyphenols) tea also contains other substances which are very important to the human organism.

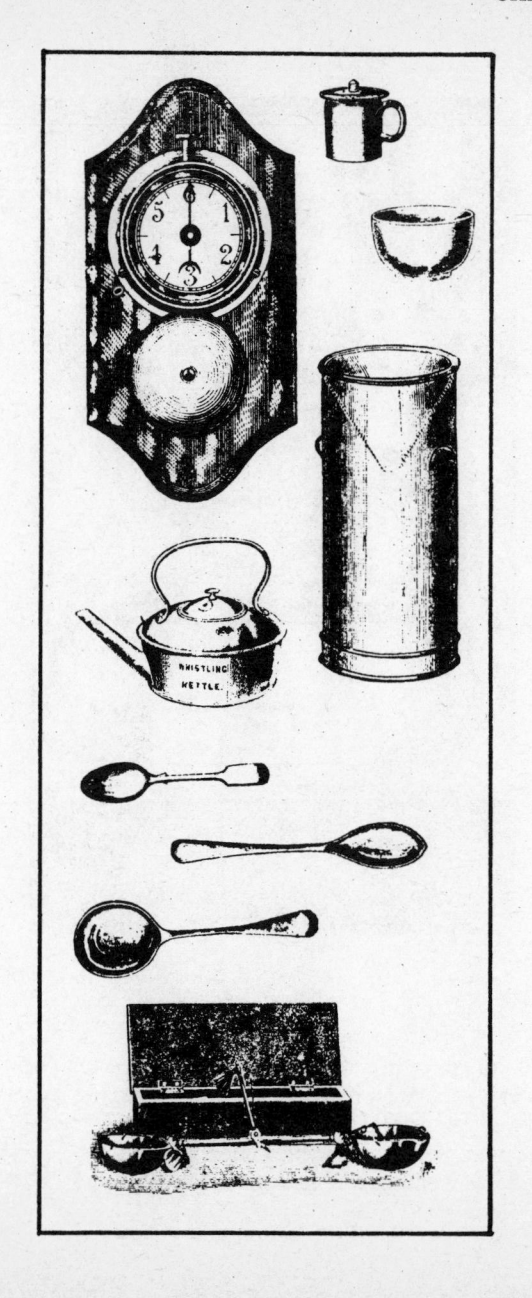

1.   The Essential Oils: Some scientists claim that these have an even stronger stimulating effect than caffeine.

2.   From the vitamin B group tea contains the water soluble vitamin B1 or thiamin. Vitamin B1 has long been known as the 'growth vitamin' and also for its prophylactic action against beri-beri disease. Recent research has shown that this vitamin is essential in the long run for people involved in strenuous mental work.

The German authority Prof. Schönberg claims that B1 can make people less sensitive to the clamour and noise in their surroundings. This immediately reminds us of the Chinese saying: 'He who drinks tea forgets the noise and unrest of everyday life.' The vitamin B1 present in tea is rapidly absorbed by the body.

3.   Tea also contains chlorophyl. The effect of this substance has not been researched very well as yet.

4.   Furthermore tea contains fluoride. As a result of the controversy about the desirability of adding fluoride to drinking water it is no doubt common knowledge that fluoride prevents tooth decay or caries. It should be noted that if young children were to drink plenty of tea there would be no need at all to add fluoride to mains water!

5.   The nutritive value of tea is not very great. However this may well be seen as an advantage in these days of affluence and general concern over diet! One cup of tea contains 0.65 gm of protein, an adult needs an average of 1 gm of protein per kilogram body weight per day.

6   One cup of tea contains 4 calories, a cup of coffee 11 and a glass of milk 107 calories. An adult leading a normal active life needs between 2500 and 3000 calories per day. Tea without milk or sugar can be recommended as non-fattening. A

cup of tea with one tablespoon of milk and 1 lump of sugar contains 40 calories. Fresh (unprocessed tea leaves) are far more nutritious; this is why the Shan people of Burma chew tea leaves all day long. Let me warn you here and now against any experiments with smoking processed tea: the least serious effect that can be expected is nausea!

Finally we should pay some attention to an article in *Nature* magazine of 9th December 1967 (number 216) by Wei Young, Robert Hotovec and Arthur Romero describing their research into 'Tea and arteriosclerosis'. They had noticed that arteriosclerosis is quite rare in China and that this was related to a lower cholesterol level in the blood. They experimented with rabbits and found that if tea is drunk during or immediately after a greasy meal this prevents an increase in the seral serum lipid content (blood fat content). This then might to some extent prevent diseases of the heart and blood vessels. On the other hand there are also respectable members of the medical profession who warn against the use of large quantities of tea by heart patients.

Directions for Making Good Tea.

WE WISH TO IMPRESS UPON OUR CUSTOMERS THE FACT THAT TEA SHOULD BE MADE FROM WATER FRESHLY BOILED; WATER THAT HAS BEEN BOILING SOME TIME DOES NOT MAKE GOOD TEA. WE HAVE FOUND, FROM CONSTANT PRACTICE IN TEA TASTING, THAT IF WE USE WATER THAT HAS BEEN BOILING FOR A LONG TIME, WE DO NOT OBTAIN ANYTHING LIKE SO GOOD A CUP OF TEA AS WE DO WHEN THE WATER HAS BEEN FRESHLY BOILED. WE KNOW IT IS NOT UNUSUAL FOR THE KETTLE TO BE PUT NEAR OR ON THE FIRE DIRECTLY AFTER DINNER, AND TO REMAIN BOILING, OR HALF BOILING, FOR HOURS; SUCH WATER CAN NEVER MAKE GOOD TEA.

Although in hot weather a glass of iced tea can be very pleasant everyone knows that during a heat wave a cup or glass of hot tea is one of the best and most delicious ways of quenching thirst. To quote Dr Bontekoe: it is a miraculous drink!!

Herb Teas

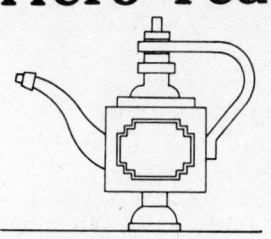

A tea trader wrote to me: 'To my mind not every infusion of dried leaves can automatically be called tea', and I am inclined to agree with him. In fact only the extract made from the leaf of *Camellia sinensis* should deserve the name tea. Why then bother with the other so-called teas in this book? Firstly, because they are for sale in specialised shops, and secondly, because their popularity is growing enormously. Furthermore they are certainly not all unpleasant, some are even quite exquisite and there are a large number which are claimed to have certain medicinal properties.

First a few hints: Never make herb teas too strong and regard the amounts given here as a maximum! Many herb teas can be blended and no doubt the shopkeeper or trader will be pleased to advise you. Herb teas are available from many chemists, nearly all health food shops and many of the addresses listed in the back of this book. Some of them you could grow or pick yourself. My personal favourites are hibiscus tea, *rooibosch* tea and lime blossom tea. Here is a list of some of the herb teas available, each with a brief description.

1.   Balm Tea (from melissa officionalis): 2 gm to one cup, don't boil. Stimulates sexual excitement.
2.   Berberis Tea: 2 gm to a cup of boiling water. For cystitis.
3.   Chamomile Tea: 1 to 2 level tablespoons of chamomile should be left to brew in a litre of boiling water for seven minutes. Sweeten to taste with honey or sugar. A traditional remedy against inflammations, toothache and period pains. It can also be used to lighten the hair.
4.   Curled Mint Tea: a deliciously refreshing tea if left to brew for five minutes. 'On the rocks': 2 parts curled mint tea to one part white Vermouth with ice cubes.
5.   Elderflower Tea: Pour one cup of boiling water on a teaspoon of dried flowers and boil for ten minutes. Against gout.
6.   Ginseng Tea is available in bags and extremely expensive. It is made from the ginseng root and imported from South Korea. It is claimed to have extraordinary powers; whilst the South Koreans were involved in the Vietnam war the state ensured by means of a monopoly that sufficient quantities were supplied. It is supposed to be an excellent remedy against impotency and I would much prefer the use of ginseng to that of the ground horn of the now very rare rhinoceros.
7.   Hemp nettle Tea: from the *Galeopsis segetum*. 1 tablespoon to one cup of water will facilitate urinating.
8.   Hibiscus Tea: from the hibiscus or rose

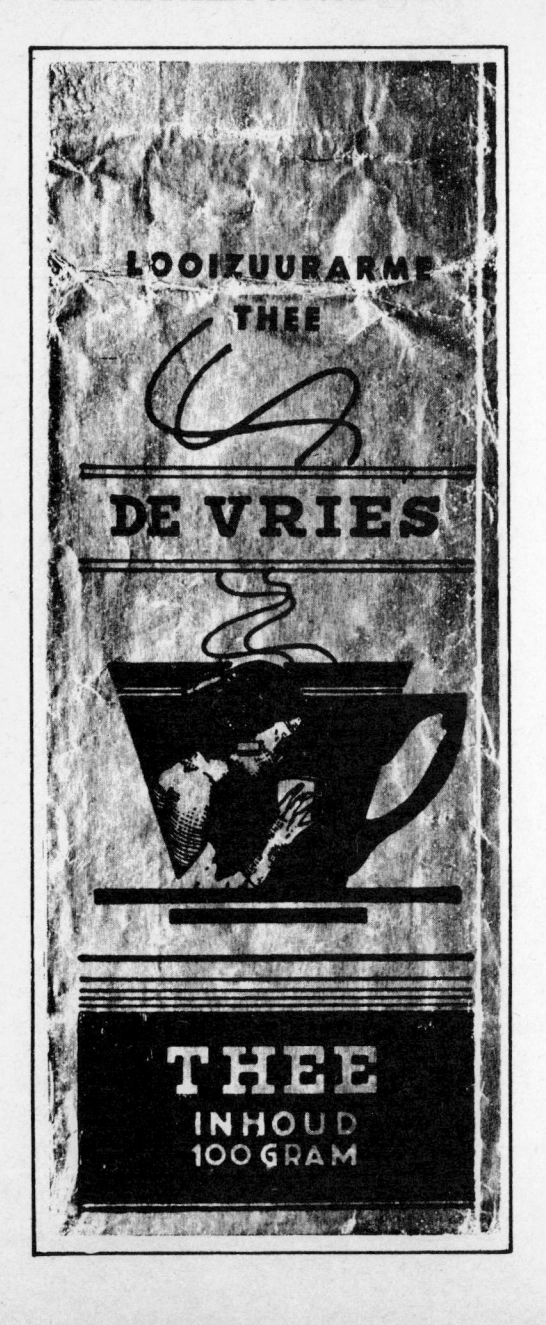

LOOIZUURARME
THEE

DE VRIES

THEE
INHOUD
100 GRAM

mallow comes from the Sudan and is one of the most popular herb teas. It should be boiled for three minutes. It can be drunk warm with a tablespoon of honey and a peppermint leaf, but the very refreshing, slightly acid taste comes out very well when it is drunk cold. It is rich in essential oils and vitamin C.

9.   Lavender Tea: This is an ideal bedtime drink as it induces sleep. It is made by pouring 1 cup of boiling water on 2 gm of dried flower.

10. Lime Blossom Tea: pour 1 litre of water on 2 level tablespoons of lime blossoms. Leave it to brew for five to seven minutes and pour out through a sieve. For alleviation of headaches and colds and stimulation of sexual excitement.

11. Marijuana Tea: In Britain, as in most other countries, the use of this is prohibited by law, and in some countries the penalties on its use are severe. However, according to experts, drinking is preferable to smoking.

12. Marjoram Tea: 2 gm of the herb to a cup of boiling water. Good against colic.

13. Maté or Yerba Maté is made from the dried leaves of the *Ilex paraguarensis*. As the name suggests Paraguay is the main supplier. The dictator Stroesner made his fortune from maté. The caffeine content is around 1.5%. In the Argentine 140,000 tons are consumed per annum. It is drunk through a straw or silver tube from a cask which hangs on the hip.

14. Rattail Plantain Tea: Pour 1 cup of boiling water on 2 gm of rattail plantain leaves. Against haemorrhoids.

15. Rooibosch Tea: Comes from the *Cyclopia genistoides* and the *Cyclopia vogelii,* two desert crops grown in the Cape province of South Africa. The instructions on the packet read—First pour boiling water on the leaves and allow to stand for

half a minute. Drain off and then pour on boiling water a second time. Add warm milk and sugar to taste.

16. Rosehip Tea: 1 teaspoon to a cup of boiling water, leave it to brew for 10 minutes and add sugar and honey to taste.

17. Rose Petal Tea: is drunk in Bulgaria. The fragrance of the rose captured in a glass!

18. Shepherd's Purse Tea: the freshly picked plants should be left to brew in simmering water for 2 hours. A remedy against period pains and the various discomforts associated with the menopause.

19. Stinging Nettle Tea: 2 gm of dried stinging nettles in 1 cup of boiling water. Against inflammation of the urinal passages.

20. Three year Tea, from Japan, is really an exception to this list as it is derived from the real tea plant but it contains only certain leaves and stems which, as the name suggests, are picked after three years of growth. The caffeine content is very low: 0.5%.

21. Walnut leaf Tea: 2 gm of dried walnut leaves to one cup of boiling water. A remedy for glandular diseases and diarrhoea.

The Latest Developments in the Tea Trade

The information in this chapter has been updated as far as possible, that is to say up till the middle of 1980. The book entitled *Tea for the British* by D.M. Forrest (see bibliography) was published in 1973 before the energy crisis had really begun. This makes Forrest's statements all the more prophetic when he writes that he can envisage a situation in which the tea-producing countries, like the oil-producing countries, will flex their muscles and force the rich countries to pay considerably more for their tea. Quite a remarkable thing to say at that time, as the price of tea had remained very stable over the period from 1963 to 1973. During those ten years it was a buyer's market i.e. the consumers were dictating the terms. After 1973 the picture gradually changed. Tea is now no longer very cheap, although it is still relatively cheap. We are now dealing rather with a seller's market (i.e. the power in the market place has shifted to the side of the producers). Why has the situation at the auctions in London, Calcutta, Cochin, Colombo and Mombasa changed so drastically? One of the main reasons is the oil crisis. The driers at the tea factory require large amounts of energy, and transport, too, has become far more expensive. (Indonesia is the only country which exports both tea and oil, but there are several other reasons

which prevent the Indonesian economy from flourishing.) In all the other tea-producing countries of the Third World, the import of oil is an ever-increasing burden on the economy. In contrast, the OPEC countries have more and more capital at their disposal. Islamic countries are traditionally tea-drinking nations. Because of this the position of countries like Saudi Arabia, Libya, Iraq and (at least until 1979) Iran, on the tea market has been very strong and has meant serious competition for the West. During the 70s, the problem was aggravated by the central position of England in the tea trade. As all prices are expressed in pounds sterling, they had to be continually adjusted. As a result of the ailing British economy, even the large and well-established British firms were sometimes forced to live from day to day. I have already mentioned competition from the Arabs. Other relative newcomers to the market such as the Soviet Union and Australia also became increasingly more aggressive in their buying behaviour. In 1977, the market was seriously disturbed by the international coffee crisis. For various reasons (harvest failure in Brazil, war in Angola, the oil crisis) coffee prices had risen astronomically. This caused a world-wide rush on tea, pushing the price of this drink up too. The cost of a reasonable

Ceylon tea rose from 110p per kilo in January 1977 to 330p in April the same year. Those wild fluctuations have fortunately subsided again. Early in 1980 prices for main season Dimbula tea (from Ceylon) varied from 140 new pence for the poorer qualities to 230 pence for the finest. In mid 1980 the average was just over 100 pence. In *Sri Lanka* the tea plantations were nationalised by the government in 1975. In view of the approaching nationalisation, the previous years had seen less fertilisation or replanting with new and better bushes. Unlike the East African countries, the Sri Lankan government has implemented a high export levy—which is however, mainly used for reinvestment in the tea production. The tea trade still constitutes 65% of the country's economy. For its finest qualities, Ceylon can still get a good price; in fact the demand for these is rising. The main buyers of top quality Ceylon tea are West Germany and Australia. Other customers for this particular line are South Africa and Russia (for their respective elites). The price level for the lesser varieties is rising too. 'Below best' and 'Medium' qualities seem to remain fairly stable. In 1979, tea exports from Sri Lanka totalled 187, 545,000 kg (slightly lower than in previous years). In 1979 the export was divided as follows:

1.	United Kingdom	21.6%
2.	Pakistan	18.6%
3.	Iraq	16.7%
4.	Egypt	14.8%
5.	United States	14.5%
6.	Syria	10.7%
7.	Saudi Arabia	8.7%
8.	Iran	7.8%
9.	Kuwait	7.0%
10.	Tunisia	6.5%
11.	Australia	5.8%
12.	South Africa	5.1%

The largest company, Lipton Ceylon, services America and Pakistan, Brooke Bond Ceylon deals with Australia and Canada, the Sri Lanka Trading Corporation ships to Iraq and Egypt. The Akhbar Brothers are responsible for Iran and Saudi Arabia, Harrison and Crossfield ship to Iraq and England. Heath & Co deal with Ireland and Holland and M.J.F. Exports with Russia and England. The Janata Estates Development Board and the States Plantation Corporation, apart from the usual supply for the Columbo auction, ship exclusively to the auctions in London. *Bangladesh* has an export tax on tea of 8.25 pence per kilogram. In 1979 production stood at 39,000 tons of which at least 30,000 was exported. The market in Pakistan, which before the war that separated the two countries used to be supplied by Bangladesh (then East Pakistan), is now entirely in the hands of Sri Lanka and Indonesia. In *India*, an export tax of no less than 40 pence per kilogram was introduced in 1977 by the government of the day. Its purpose was to protect the growing home market. These measures have been maintained by Mrs Gandhi's Congress Party which came to power in 1980. About 40% of the world's tea comes from India. In 1977, India's share in the export trade was 29%. There are large-scale plans for the expansion of the tea acreage in Southern India, but progress in this direction is slow, and the quality of the tea produced here still leaves a lot to be desired. Dooars tea from northern India has more character. West Germany in particular is prepared to pay high prices for a good quality Assam tea. At the moment it looks very likely that the 1980 harvest in Assam will be excellent. There are, however, political problems. The native Naga population in Assam feels threatened by the insurgence of poor 'Bengalis'. In many places this has already led to armed resistance. The transport of the oil found in Assam has been successfully blocked by the rebellious Nagas. They are threatening to do the same with tea and jute transports. In Darjeeling the problems are of quite a different nature. Data from the India Tea Association shows that the total area of Darjeeling gardens has dropped from 20,000 hectares (just under 50,000 acres) to 14,000 hectares (about 35,000 acres). The average yield per hectare is still 600 kilograms compared with a national average of 1500 kilograms. Nearly 80% of the bushes are over 50 years old, whilst labour productivity has dropped from 268 to 248 kilograms per annum over the last 10 years. A lot of medium quality Darjeeling tea still goes to the Soviet Union. Only the West Germans are prepared to pay high prices for top quality first flush Darjeeling. In the *People's Republic of China* more tea is grown now than ever before. The quality of exported tea is improving all the time and the quantity is growing too; the Chinese exported 30,000 tons in 1970, compared with 53,000 tons in 1975. *Turkey* now drinks most of its inferior product itself. 90% of the 117,000 tons grown is for home consumption. Excellent!

Finally *Indonesia*; here the tea is grown on vast estates as well as by small farmers on little plots of land. The plantations produce 50,000 tons per annum on average and the smallholders 15,000 tons. The three state plantation groups, one in North Sumatra, and two in West Java, supply about half of the total Indonesian export. The Indonesian position in the Australian and American markets is very strong. Indonesia keeps its prices

artifically high. In May, 1980, a conference of tea-producing countries was held at Bandung in Indonesia where world export quotas were established. The aim is for a minimum export price of 105 new pence by the year 1985. The average price for 1979 was 94 pence.

Uganda has been given some leeway by the other tea countries to enable it to regain part of the position lost during the dictatorship of Idi Amin. An encouraging sign is the revival of the International Tea Committee. One half of its costs is borne by the Western countries the rest contributed by the tea exporting countries. In 1980 the International Tea Promotion Association (ITPA) was set up in Rotterdam. The ITPA has nine member countries controlling 90% of the tea market.

Let's now have a look at developments among the consumers, limiting the account to a few EEC countries. First of all *Great Britain*. In 1978, the tea consumption per head of population was 3600 g. The British tea market is still the largest in the world, worth around 300 million pounds sterling. We are talking about a consumption of 200,000 tons per annum (the total world production in 1977 was 886,000 tons). In 1977, Great Britain imported 33% of its total tea imports from India, 17% from Kenya, 10% from Sri Lanka and 6% from Malawi. In England, tea accounts for 70% of all hot drinks consumed.

The introduction of the tea bag actually caused a drop in the nation's overall consumption of tea during the 60s because less fannings (used in tea bags) are needed per litre of tea than are needed for leaf tea (used in packet tea). Consumption rates went up again temporarily during 1977 when coffee became prohibitively expensive. The four main brands cover 80% of the market. The profit margins on this tea are extremely small, because the large supermarket chains compete with each other through special offers. To keep the tea cheap for the housewife the manufacturers economise on quality. In this context an article entitled 'Which Tea' in the *Sunday Times Magazine* of March 30, 1980, was very revealing. A number of people interested in food (not professional tea experts) were allowed to taste different teas under expert guidance. Whilst amateur wine tasters can apparently make the most awful blunders, this group of tea tasters had little trouble recognising quality. Only one top quality Assam tea remained unappreciated. Very little praise, however, could be found for the big-selling supermarket brands; 'bitter, disgusting, terrible, vicious, repulsive, tastes of straw,' were some of the opinions given. The professional tea taster present limited himself (tongue in cheek) to the statement that these were 'typical UK blends'. Of course,

good tea *is* available in England. You only have to look at the food departments of stores like Harrods, Selfridges and Fortnum & Mason. (For specialist shops see under addresses.)

Next *The Netherlands*. After the War, tea drinking in the Netherlands gradually declined. This downward trend was halted in 1969; since then tea consumption has grown at the steady rate of 5% per year. This increase was much more pronounced in 1977, the year when coffee became ridiculously expensive. Since then there has been a slight fall followed by stabilisation. In 1979 tea consumption per head of population was 637g. The Dutch market requires average, medium quality tea; mainly blends of various origins. Specialities are sold by about twenty-five shops and their share of the market comes to roughly 4%. The consumption of teas with an added aroma is expected to rise. Their present share of the market is still below 1%. In 1979, about 80% of the tea in the Netherlands was sold in bags and 20% in packets. (The more expensive tins accounted for approximately 1%) *Belgium* has always been an undeveloped 'tea country' though matters improved a little during the 70's. In 1971, consumption was just below 51g per head of population. In 1978, a total of 750 tonnes was consumed; 75g per head of population. The present fashion is for expensive tea in tins. No less than 10% of tea is sold in tins. The capriciousness of fashion has also favoured tea in *France* during the last few years. In 1964 the French consumed 1500 tonnes, in 1978 this grew to 5000 tonnes. On top of that, quite remarkably, France consumed another 1700 tons of green tea from China in 1978. This is probably mostly drunk by North African immigrants. About half of the black tea comes from Ceylon. Tins (especially Earl Grey tea) are in great demand; no less than 20% of all tea sold. Tea bags account for 48% and packets for 18% of the consumption. The remainder (14%) is sold loose over the counter. The market for herb teas ('infusions') in France is about 50% larger than the market for real tea. Herb teas are drunk by people from all walks of life, whereas 'real' tea is mostly drunk by the well-to-do and/or the intelligensia.

Although *Germany* is traditionally a coffee-drinking nation, tea has become fashionable there too. This has been noted by the author as the German translation of this book sells very well! In the Federal Republic the average tea consumption per head of population in 1967 was 134g. In 1977 this had risen to 210g though the consumption pattern in East Friesland still differs greatly. In 1977, consumption there was 3100g per head, not far below the level of consumption per capita in England. Nearly 40% of all imported tea comes from India and a further 20% from Ceylon. The market is divided as follows: special blends (Ceylon tea, China blends tea) 65–70%, cheaper strong blends (for instance for East Friesland) 15–20%. Tea with added aromas 10%. Top qualities (again for East Friesland mainly) 5%. Tea bags account for 55%, packets for 30% and tins for 10%, loose tea 5%. Herb tea has always been in great demand in Germany. The ratio of black tea in bags to herb tea in bags is about 40–60.

Reconstruction of a North Afghan tea house in the Rijksmuseum for Ethnology in Leiden.

Addresses and Literature

First of all some useful addresses. London still boasts a few establishments where one can take a good old-fashioned afternoon tea: selected China or India tea accompanied by assorted sandwiches and cakes served between 4 and 6 in the afternoon. Tea at the Ritz in Piccadilly is supposed to be a very worthwhile experience, and the Strand Palace Hotel is also famous for its tea.

William Fortnum was employed by Queen Anne. Together with Mason he started a business which developed into the famous department store Fortnum & Mason in Piccadilly. An excellent tea is served there between 3.30 and 5.30. Besides afternoon tea, the Ceylon Tea Centre, 22 Regent Street, also offers a wide variety of information on tea. Then there is the Tea Board of India, situated at 343–349 Oxford Street. For all possible and impossible information one should contact the Tea Council Ltd, (Middle Block) (First Floor), Sir John Lyon House, 5 High Timber Street, London EC4V 3NJ.

For larger quantities of tea at reduced prices the following addresses might be useful:

Wittard, 111 Fulham Road, SW3
Culpeper Ltd., 3 East Bury Street, SW1
Algerian Coffee (they sell tea too!) 52 Old Compton Street, W1.

Richmond Tea and Coffee Co., 9 Hill Rise, Richmond Upon Thames.
Moore Bros., 166 Notting Hill Gate, London W11.

In Scotland:
Young & Saunders, 5 Queensferry Street, Edinburgh EH2 4PD.
In this shop, time has stood still since Victorian days!

In Ireland:
Bewley's Tea and Coffee, 78 Grafton Street, Dublin
The Georgian Shop, 54 William Street, Dublin

Literature

All About Tea, William H. Ukers. Published by The Tea and Coffee Trade Journal Co., New York.

The Culture and Marketing of Tea, C.R. Harler. Oxford U.P. London 1963.

Tea and Coffee, Edward Bramah. Hutchinson of London, London 1972.

Tea for the British, D.M. Forrest. Chatto & Windus, London 1973.

Tea, the Colonial Legacy, J. Hamilton. T. Lawrence etc.,Cambridge World Development Action Group, Cambridge 1976.

Tea Ceremony Utensils, Fujioka, Weatherhill Co., New York.

The Art of Chabana, Flower of the Tea Ceremony, Mittwer, Tuttle and Co., Vermont/Tokyo 1977.

Tea Processing, J. Werkhoven, F.A.O. Agricultural Services Bulletin no. 26, Roma 1974.

Tea, T. Eden, Tropical Agricultural Series. Longman, London 1976.

The World Tea Economy, G.K. Sarkar, Oxford U.P., Delhi 1972.

A Hundred Years of Ceylon Tea, D.M. Forrest, Chatto & Windus, London.

A History of the Indian Tea Industry, Sir Percival Griffiths, Weidenfeld & Nicolson, London 1967.

Tea Manufacture in Ceylon, E.L. Keegel, reprint, Monographs on tea-production in Ceylon no. 4, De la Salle Press, Colombo 1965.

One Day Course in Tea Manufacture, E.L. Keegel, monograph no. 5, Colombo 1963.

The Tea Cookbook, William J Kaufman, Double-day and Co., New York 1966.

Zen and Japanese Culture, Suzuki, New York 1959.

The Tea Ceremony, Tanaka, Kodansha Int. Ltd., Tokyo & New York 1973.

Tea Ceremony, Iguchi, tr. Clark, Color Books Hoikusha, Osaka 1979.

Tea Taste in Japanese Art, Lee, Asia House 1976.

The Way of Tea, Castile, Weatherhill, New York 1971.

The Classic of Tea, Lu Yü, tr. Carpenter, Little Brown and Co., Boston 1974.

The Tea Story, J.M. Scott, Heinemann, London 1964.

Tea, Jamie Shalleck, Viking Press, New York 1972.

The Tea Book, Serena Hardy, Whittet Books, London 1979.

The Book of Coffee and Tea, Joel, David & Karl Shapira, St. James Press London 1975.

Tea-cup Fortune Telling, signs illustrated and simply explained by Minetta, W. Foulsham & Co., London 1972.

The Bird of Dawning, John Edward Masefield, 1933.

The Log of the Cutty Sark, Basil Lubbock.

The Cutty Sark, Noel C.L. Hackney.

The Cutty Sark, C. Nepean Longridge.

London Coffee Houses, Bryant Lillywhite, London 1963.

The Book of Tea, Kakuzo Okakura, Ed. & Intro. by Everett F. Bleiler, Dover Publ. Inc., New York.

Chinoiserie, the Vision of Cathay, Hugh Honour, London, 1973.

Talking of Teapots, John Bedford, Parrish, London 1964.

Coffee Pots and Tea Pots for the Collector, Henry Sandon, Bartholomew & Son, Edinburgh 1973.

Japanese Arts and the Tea Ceremony, Tatsusaburo Hayashiya, Masao Nakamura, Seizo Hayashiya. Tr. & adapt. by Joseph Macadan, The Heibonsha Survey of Japanese Art, Vol. 15, Weatherhill Inc., New York 1974.

Quotations

So much has been said and written about tea that you could probably write a complete book of quotations on the subject. There are Chinese poems, Japanese haiku's, cosy middle class rhymes, passages in world literature ranging from *Alice in Wonderland* to the *Pickwick Papers* in which a meeting of teetotallers is described. I have here limited myself to some poetry. First of all from China a poem by Po-Chu-I, eminently translated into English by Arthur Waley.

On Rising Late

All the morning I have lain perversely in bed,
Now at dusk I rise with many yawns.
My warm stove is quick to get a blaze,
At the cold mirror I am slow in doing my hair.
With melted snow I boil fragrant tea,
Seasoned with curds I cook a milk pudding.
At my sloth and greed there is no one but me to laugh,
My cheerful vigour none but myself knows.
The taste of my wine is mild and works no poison,
The notes of my harp are soft and bring no sadness.
To the Three Joys in the book of Mencious
I have added the fourth of playing with my baby boy.

A poem by G. K. Chesterton (1874–1936)

Tea is like to the East he grows in
A great yellow Mandarin
With urbanity of manner
And unconsciousness of sin.

Percy Bysshe Shelley (1792–1822) wrote:

The liquid doctors rail at, and that I
will quaff in spite of them, and when I die
we'll toss up which died first of drinking tea.

The following is an English students' song:

A tea-leaf for tea-lovers,
Early morning, noon or night
A cup of tea is my delight.
When the sun is blazing hot
Boil the kettle, fill the pot.
When you're chilled by cold or rain,
Tea will warm you up again.
Let the morn rise red or grey—
Early tea should start the day.
Delicious meals can always be
Made better by a cup of tea
And when mere thought of food dismays,
This fragrant drink you still shall praise.
A perfect picnic cannot start
Without a teapot in its heart.
And when outside is fog and mire
How good is tea beside the fire!
When you're sad and all goes wrong
Make the tea and make it strong! When you're glad
you'll say with me:
Now let's have a cup of tea!

1961

T.S. Eliot. Portrait of a Lady:

Now that lilacs are in bloom
she has a bowl of lilacs in her room
and twists one in her fingers while she talks.
'Ah, my friend, you do not know,
                    you do not know
what life is, you hold it in your hands';
(slowly twisting the lilac stalks)
'You let it flow from you.
                    you let it flow,
and youth is cruel, and has no remorse
and smiles at situations which it cannot see.'
I smile, of course,
and go on drinking Tea.

Ezra Pound. The Tea Shop:

The girl in the tea shop
        is not so beautiful as she was,
the August has worn against her–
She does not get up the stairs to eagerly;
yes, she also will turn middle-aged,
and the glow of youth that she spread about us
        as she brought us our muffins
will be spread about us no longer.
She also will turn middle-aged.

Edward Lear:

There was an old man of Dumbree,
who taught little owls to drink tea;
for he said, 'To eat mice, is not proper or nice.'
That amiable man of Dumbree.

An advertisement showing from left to right; Gladstone, Florence Nightingale and Baroness Burdett Couts

Edmund Waller's 'Of Tea Commended by Her Majesty', 1663:

> Venus her Myrtle, Phoebus has her bays;
> Tea both excels, which she vouchsafe to praise.
> The best of Queens, and best of herbs, we owe
> To that bold nation, which the way did show
> To the fair regions where the sun doth rise,
> Whose rich production we so justly prize.
> The Muse's friend, tea doth our fancy aid,
> Repress those vapours which the head invade,
> And keep the palace of the soul serene,
> Fit on her birthday to salute the Queen.

Chances are the tea was better than the poetry.

Johnson described himself as 'a hardened and shameless tea-drinker, who has, for twenty years, diluted his meals with only the infusion of this fascinating plant; whose kettle has scarcely time to cool; who with tea amuses the evening, with tea solaces the midnight, and, with tea, welcomes the morning'.

Marie Trevelyan writing about Wales in 1892: "The hill women are fond of drinking tea in immoderate quantities and that is why their complexions fade early and leave a sallow and muddy colour upon the skin ... The teapot is always on the hob and there is no end to the potations."

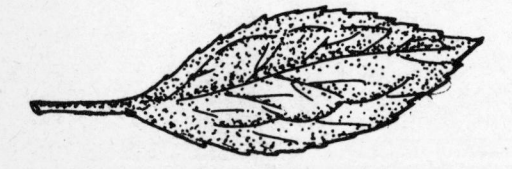

Robert Chambers, 'Domestic Annals of Scotland':

"For some years the use of tea had been creeping in amongst nearly all ranks of the people. It was thought by many reflecting persons, amongst whom was the enlightened Lord President Forbes, to be in many respects an improper diet, expensive, wasteful of time, and calculated to render the population weakly and effeminate. During the course of this year, there was a vigorous movement all over Scotland for getting the use of tea abated. Towns, parishes, and countries passed resolutions condemnatory of the Chinese leaf, and pointing strongly to the manlier attractions of beer. The tenants of William Fullarton, of Fullarton, in Aryshire, in a bond they entered into on the occasion, thus delivered themselves: 'We, being all farmers by profession, think it needless to restrain ourselfes formally from indulging in that foreign and consumptive luxury called tea; for when we consider the *slender constitutions* of many of higher rank, amongst whom it is used, we conclude that it would be but an improper diet to quality us for the more *robust* and *manly* parts of our business; and therefore we shall only give our testimony against it, and leave the enjoyment of it altogether to those who can afford to be *weak, indolent,* and *useless.*' "

Lewis Carroll, 'Alice in Wonderland':

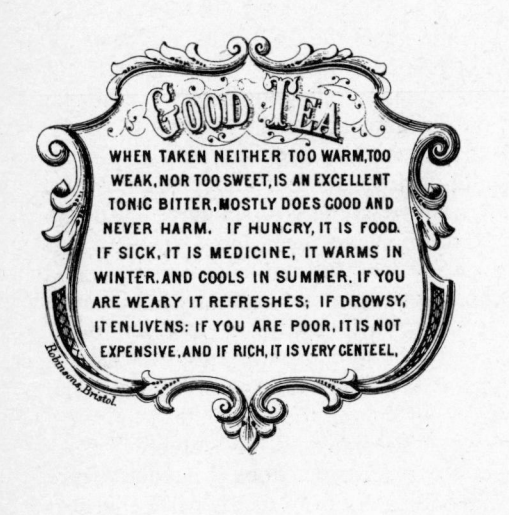

GOOD TEA

WHEN TAKEN NEITHER TOO WARM, TOO
WEAK, NOR TOO SWEET, IS AN EXCELLENT
TONIC BITTER, MOSTLY DOES GOOD AND
NEVER HARM. IF HUNGRY, IT IS FOOD.
IF SICK, IT IS MEDICINE, IT WARMS IN
WINTER, AND COOLS IN SUMMER. IF YOU
ARE WEARY IT REFRESHES; IF DROWSY,
IT ENLIVENS: IF YOU ARE POOR, IT IS NOT
EXPENSIVE, AND IF RICH, IT IS VERY GENTEEL,

And hundreds of voices joined in the chorus:
"Then fill up the glasses as quick as you can,
and sprinkle the table with buttons and bran:
put cats in the coffee, and mice in the tea–
and welcome Queen Alice with thirty-times-three!"
Then followed a confused noise of cheering, and
Alice thought to herself, "Thirty times three makes
ninety.
I wonder if anyone's counting?" In a minute there
was silence again, and the same shrill voice sang
another verse:
"O looking glass creatures, quoth Alice, draw near!
'Tis an honour to see me, a favour to hear:
'Tis a privilege high to have dinner and tea
along with the Red Queen, the White Queen, and
me!"

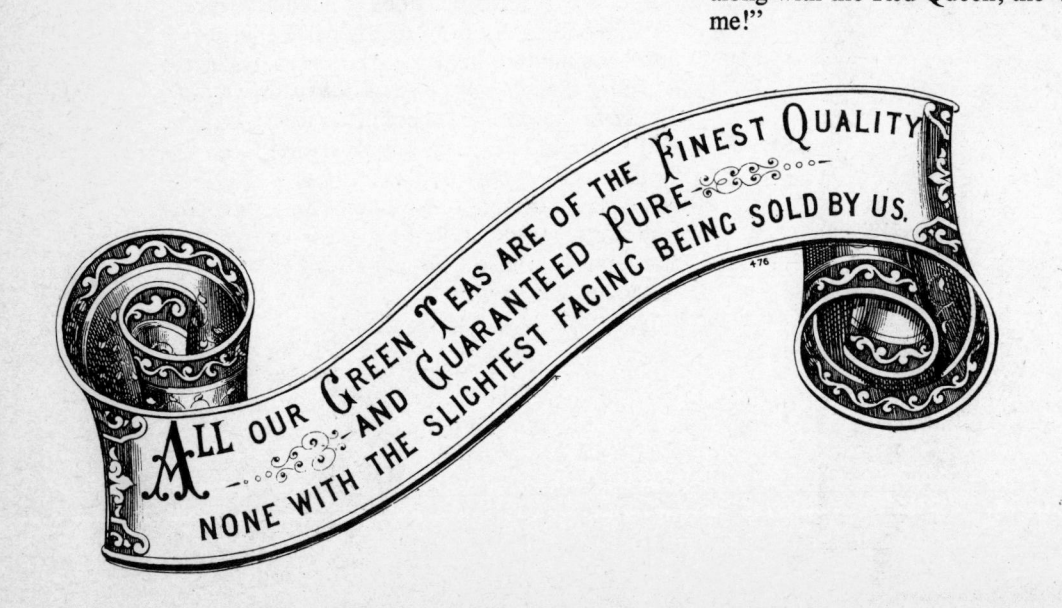

ALL OUR GREEN TEAS ARE OF THE FINEST QUALITY AND GUARANTEED PURE NONE WITH THE SLIGHTEST FACING BEING SOLD BY US.

Dr. Thomas Short, 'Discourses upon Tea' 1750:

'There is scarce any Distemper for which Nature provide us not with infinitely better and surer Help from other Vegetables.'

and

'Such as lead an idle and sedentary Life, should either drink little, or have it pretty strong and seldom, to compensate, in some measure, their want of due Exercise; but hard working laborious People have nothing to do with it; they want a Liquor that stays longer in the Body, elevates and nourishes more. I would likewise dissuade from using it, all that feel a great Coldness in the Stomach and whole Belly, so as to cause Shivering after it; and when it occasions a Paleness, a faint discoloured Look, nocturnal Pains, Numbness of the Hands, Dimness of Sight, Lowness of Spirit, Want of Sleep, Loss of Appetite, Weakness and Leanness, etc. To all these may be added, the too common pernicious Custom of drinking it with volatile Spirits, Drams, etc. The last Disorders are no Exceptions to a moderate Use of Tea in general; for with how many Persons do Milk, Ale, Drams, Cheese, and many other Meats and Drinks disagree, yet all of them are good, and do well with such as they agree with. Nor is it possible to say beforehand, with what healthy Persons Tea will disagree, till they have used it; where it disagrees, it should immediately be left off; for there is no altering or compelling a Constitution. However, where it agrees, it excels all other Vegetables foreign or domestick, for preventing Sleepiness, Drowsiness, or Dulness, and taking off Weariness of Fatigue, raising the Spirits safely, corroborating the Memory, strengthening the Judgement, quickening the Invention, etc. but then it should be drank moderately, and in the Afternoon chiefly, and not made too habitual.'

ROBINSONS BRISTOL

Index